CYPRUS

By the staff of Editions Berlitz

How to use our guide

- All the **practical information,** hints and tips that you will need before and during the trip start on p. 102, with a complete list of contents on p. 105.

- For **general background,** see the sections Cyprus and the Cypriots, p. 6, and A Brief History, p. 14.

- All the principal **sights** to visit are described between pp. 28 and 85. Our own choice of sights most highly recommended is pinpointed by the Berlitz traveller symbol.

- **Sports** and **leisure activities** are described between pp. 86 and 89.

- A rundown of suggestions of **purchases** to look out for is on pp. 90–92.

- **Nightlife, Festivals** and **Events** figure between pp. 92 and 95.

- Finally, the pleasures and possibilities of **eating out** in Cyprus are covered between pp. 96 and 101.

- An **index** on pp. 127–128 lists the place names occurring in the guide.

Text: Suzanne Patterson
Photography: Jürg Donatsch
Layout: Philippe Aquoise
We are very grateful to Beatrice Power and Anna-Lena Bergkvist for their help in the preparation of this guide. Our thanks also go to Kostas Loizu and the Cyprus Hotel Association. Cyprus Air and the Cyprus Tourism Organization in Nicosia and Zurich, particularly Heide Boller, also provided valuable assistance.
Cartography: Falk-Verlag, Hamburg.

Cover picture: Monastery of Ayia Napa
Photo pp. 2–3: Ayios Yeoryios near Paphos

Contents

Cyprus and the Cypriots

If love is irresistible, so is Aphrodite's island—as Cyprus has been known since antiquity. Impressed by the natural beauty, charm and easygoing island pace, most visitors agree that this is truly a fitting dwelling place for the goddess of love. The romantic side of Cyprus has inspired poets and novelists through the centuries—from Homer to Lawrence Durrell, whose reflective essay *Bitter Lemons* (1957) is the classic modern work on Cyprus.

Tucked into the easternmost corner of the Mediterranean, 45 miles south of Turkey and 60 miles west of Syria, Cyprus is the third largest Mediterranean island after Sicily and Sardinia. It covers an area of 3,572 square miles, but it never feels big. Landscapes can change quickly as you drive along, and the seashore is never more than an hour or two away.

All is not idyllic, however. For Cyprus is a divided nation. The Attila Line boundary splits the island nearly in half, with the self-declared, independent Turkish Republic of Northern Cyprus, and the Greek-Cypriot Republic of Cyprus to the south. For the time being, the border between north and south remains closed. Visitors to Greek Cyprus may not cross over to the Turkish side and vice versa. We concentrate here mainly on the Republic of Cyprus, still easy to visit, most hospitable and very scenic.

Like many Mediterranean islands, Cyprus has a past fraught with battles, conquests and drama. It was populated

as far back as 5,800 B.C. and is therefore a layered storehouse of archaeological treasure that continues to yield up new discoveries.

Phoenicians and Assyrians, Greeks, Egyptians and Persians all held sway over Cyprus. The Romans were in charge for several centuries; the Byzantines, Lusignans and Venetians had their say later. The Turks and Islam reigned for 300 years—until the British took over in 1878. Even today, with independence (granted in 1960), Great Britain retains sovereign military bases on the south coast, and the influence of Britain remains strong. Most Cypriots speak English—some with a perfect Oxford accent. Road signs are in both Greek and English. Driving is on the

What could possibly be so fascinating to young and old alike?

Rugged pine-clad mountains, golden beaches: scenery to please all.

left, and many people perpetuate the afternoon tea ritual.

Nicosia, an old-new city, has been capital of Cyprus since the 12th century. It rises up out of the Messaoria Plain, arid and sizzling in summer, carpeted with flowers in the spring. To the north are the hazy violet slopes of the Kyrenia mountain chain, scattered with Gothic castles.

To the west barren hills and plains give way to the wooded heights of the Troodos mountains, adequately snow-clad in winter for skiing. In summer cool mountain streams thread their way down the lower slopes, and the valleys are redolent with the scents of herbs, flowers and fruit from the orchards. The Troodos area is the site of dozens of monasteries in the Byzantine-Greek Orthodox style; many are pilgrimage shrines and most welcome overnight guests.

There are different ways to get around the island; if you're daring and enjoy a little danger as a spice of life, you'll drive yourself around some of the difficult mountain roads to see Cyprus's venerable monaste-

ries. But there are also taxis
—both private and shared vehicles, the latter a speciality of
Cyprus—and excellent bus tours
of the high spots to spare you the
do-it-yourself pains.

To the south of the island are
most of the best beaches, the
resort towns and the vineyards.
Sightseeing highlights include
the charming city of Larnaca
with ancient ruins and a good
museum; the boom-town of Limassol, whose festivals (especially wine) are legendary; and
Paphos, perhaps the prettiest
beachside resort. Noted for its
stunning Roman mosaics and
fabulous rock tombs, Paphos
has a lazy, unspoiled air that

belies the slick new, low-rise
buildings. The south coast
offers spectacular views and
Greco-Roman sites, as well as
the Birthplace of Aphrodite.
And the Baths of Aphrodite,
to the north near Polis, is one
of the most ravishing spots in
the Mediterranean.

But don't neglect the pleasures of the table—a big part of
the fun on the island. Whether
you choose a little café-taverna
or a sophisticated restaurant,
you'll find a wealth of dishes
that draw inspiration from
Greece and the Levant. The
hors d'oeuvres or *mezedes* are
sometimes so copious and
varied you can make more **9**

than a meal out of them, while the excellent Cypriot wine adds extra enjoyment for everybody who likes to indulge in a touch of the grape.

Even more engaging and heartening than these sensual delights are the people—with an exuberant Greek-Mediterranean mélange in their background, and a modicum of British decorum for contrast. The clichés of Zorba-style dress and raucous behaviour are alien to this island, where people are dignified and yet cheerful. On the whole, Cypriots are among the most civilized people in the Western world—if by civilized one means not only an awareness of history and culture, but also real kindness and consideration. Cypriots are innately well-mannered.

However, brooding resentments sometimes surface through their outward aplomb. Greek Cypriots feel that the Turkish population (18 per cent of the island's total) is unfairly occupying 37 per cent of the land. Many Greek-Cypriot refugees now living in the south have been displaced from homes, property and careers in the north, while relatively few Turkish Cypriots were adversely affected by partition. But Greek Cypriots have shown themselves energetic in the pursuit of new work and a new life, and they're unfailingly gracious to foreign visitors.

"Where are you from?", is the inevitable and altogether friendly Cypriot question, whether asked by a museum guard, tourist office representative, a waiter or an ice-cream vendor. They aren't being impertinent; they really want to know and hope to strike up a conversation. It's rare that a visitor can depart without entering into a chat, accepting a coffee or, perhaps, a gift of fruit or cakes. Cypriot hospitality is enveloping, but of the most ingenuous kind.

Yet open as Cypriots are to strangers, a closely knit family life takes precedence here. Strict rituals are observed for such occasions as baptism or marriage. Weddings are planned by both families down to the last detail of protocol and decor. Greek Orthodoxy is an intangible presence in most families, observed faithfully, especially by the distaff side; it is the women who attend services, light votive candles and venerate icons.

The Republic of Cyprus is not exactly rich, but it's not poor either. Nobody starves, filth and beggars are practically unknown, as is crime, at least as perpetrated by local people.

And lightheartedness is the prevalent theme. Because the Cypriots are gregarious, everybody else becomes so as well, and tourists meet and make friends as a matter of course.

Newcomers rush around sightseeing—trying to fit in all the archaeological sites, museums and monasteries. But if you feel overwhelmed by it all, you can always retire to a nearby café, and the beach is never far away. Sporting people love the surfing, snorkelling, sailing and water-skiing. Tennis is available all over, and the mountains are superb for summer hiking.

The Aphrodite aspect of Cyprus may appeal to lovers young or old, but it's really love of life—*joie de vivre*—that sets the mood on this entrancing, multi-faceted island.

Waiting for action: nets and fishermen's boats, Polis Harbour.

Landmark Events

B.C.

5,800	Neolithic settlements established
1,400	Mycenaean merchants found city-kingdoms
c. 800	Phoenicians settle at Kition
546	Two centuries of Persian rule begin
333	Alexander the Great liberates Cyprus
295	Cyprus falls to the Ptolemies
58	Rome takes over

A.D.

45	St. Paul and St. Barnabas make converts to Christianity
395	Roman empire divided, Cyprus falls within Eastern empire
488	Autonomy of the Church of Cyprus confirmed
647	Saracens invade
1191	Richard I (the Lionheart) conquers Cyprus
1192	Lusignans institute feudal rule
1260	Latin (Roman Catholic) church established
1373	Genoa invades, wins Famagusta
1489	Venetian Republic in control
1570	Ottoman Turks invade, ruling Cyprus for 3½ centuries
1754	Sultan acknowledges Orthodox Archbishop as ethnarch (leader of Greek Cypriot nation)
1821	Turks quell Cypriot rising in the wake of Greek War of Independence
1878	Great Britain takes over administration of Cyprus
1914	Turkey sides with Germany in World War I, Great Britain annexes Cyprus
1925	Cyprus becomes a crown colony
1950	Makarios elected archbishop, leads struggle for *enosis*.
1955	EOKA launches campaign of violence
1958	Turkish Cypriots call for partition
1960	Cyprus wins independence on August 16, Archbishop Makarios elected president
1963	Fighting breaks out between Turkish and Greek Cypriots
1974	Turkey invades Cyprus on July 20, occupies the north of the island
1977	Archbishop Makarios dies, Spyros Kyprianou succeeds as president
1983	Turkish Cypriots unilaterally declare independence
1985	Talks on reunification convene at the United Nations in New York.

A Brief History

Primitive people of unknown origin took up residence on Cyprus as far back as the Neolithic period, around 5,800 B.C. Hunters and farmers, the first Cypriots lived in dozens of settlements, constructing beehive dwellings and fashioning tools, utensils and weapons of stone. By 2,500 B.C., copper, abundant on Cyprus, began to replace stone in implements and weapons. As an exporter of the metal, Cyprus emerged early as a trading centre of the Mediterranean.

During the Bronze Age islanders evolved different types of metalwork and pottery. Much of the latter was red-polished. Distinctive geometric styles came into fashion, and by 1,600 B.C. pottery was being shipped in quantity to Syria and Palestine. Trade sprang up between Cyprus and the Near East towards the middle of the 2nd millennium.

Early Days

But the dominant power in the Mediterranean was Egypt, to whom Cyprus paid tribute. Although the Egyptians had no settlements on the island, they did form an enthusiastic mercantile partnership with the Cypriots after 1,450 B.C. Commerce flourished, especially around Enkomi and along the east and south-east coasts. From about 1,400 to 1,250 B.C. merchants from Mycenae in Greece came to trade in Cypriot copper, their arrival on the scene firmly establishing the ascendency of the Greek language, religion and way of life. The cities they founded grew into prosperous mini-kingdoms, each ruled by a monarch.

A period of uncertainty ensued, marked by piracy and the disintegration of Bronze Age civilizations in the eastern Mediterranean (early 13th century B.C.). With recovery, elaborate temples were built (outstanding was the sanctuary of Aphrodite at Palea Paphos) and artistic activity—especially ivory carving, bronze founding, goldsmithing—burgeoned. Around 1,190 B.C. pirates attacked the coastal area, and Aegean refugees (including many Achaean Greeks) streamed into the island after the Trojan War, swelling the populations of the city-kingdoms of Salamis, Curium (Kourion), Lapithos, Cerynia (Kyrenia), Marion (now Polis), Palea Paphos and Tamassos.

A favourite scenic swimming place by the Baths of Aphrodite near Polis. The cross on the rock commemorates a diver who drowned near here.

The Iron Age

As iron was replacing bronze in the 9th century, Phoenician colonists established a city-kingdom of their own at the onetime Mycenaean centre of Kition (near today's Larnaca). They turned the more impressive of the Bronze Age temples there into sanctuaries in honour of their fertility goddess Astarte—a symbolic relative of Aphrodite, the love goddess, Cyprus's perennial favourite deity. Achaean Greeks, Phoenicians and Cypriots exchanged ideas and techniques, infusing new life into the arts. By the 8th century B.C., trade with the Aegean was booming once **15** more, and a major monument was under construction: the royal tombs of Salamis, the most powerful of Cyprus's city-kingdoms.

From 700 B.C. onwards, Cyprus was successively invaded and ruled by Assyria, Egypt and Persia. In thrall to foreign overlords, the city-kingdoms of Cyprus nevertheless kept a certain autonomy. Culturally, a strong oriental influence was brought to bear, but the Greek cause had an ardent champion in King Evagoras I of Salamis (435–374 B.C.), an ally of Athens and advocate of Hellenism. Evagoras led the struggle against the Persians and their Phoenician allies, temporarily liberating Cyprus.

It was Alexander the Great, however, who finally crushed Persian power in 333 B.C. and took Cyprus under his wing. When Alexander died a decade later, the island served as the battleground for his successors Antigonos and Ptolemy I of Egypt.

In 310 B.C. Nicocreon, the last king of Salamis, was forced by Ptolemy to commit suicide, and his family followed suit as the palace burned. After this upheaval, the centre of power shifted from Salamis to Nea Paphos. Under the Ptolemies

(295–58 B.C.), the independent city-kingdoms withered away as direct imperial rule was imposed.

Under Roman Rule

Cyprus was conquered by Rome in 58 B.C. Julius Caesar later ceded it to Ptolemy and Arsinoë of Egypt, and Antony gave it to Cleopatra. However, by A.D. 30 Rome once again gained control, and Cyprus was administered by a proconsul in the prosperous period of the

Pax Romana. Nea Paphos, still the most important city, served as capital.

In A.D. 45 Christianity came to Cyprus with that ubiquitous and persevering evangelizer, St. Paul, and his companion, St. Barnabas, a native of Salamis, who was to die a martyr on the island of his birth. In Paphos the Proconsul Sergius Paulus was converted to Christianity, making Cyprus the first country to be governed by a Christian.

Ruins above the sea at Curium testify to the site's former glory.

Outpost of Byzantium

With the ground swell of Christianity, dozens, even hundreds, of churches and monasteries were founded. Following terrible earthquakes in 332 and 342, Salamis was rebuilt as capital of Cyprus. Like Byzantium, renamed Constantinople, it took the name of **17**

the Emperor Constantine to become (for a relatively short while) Constantia. After the division of the Roman empire into eastern and western halves in 395, Cyprus remained within the orbit of the Eastern (Byzantine) empire and was ruled from Antioch in Syria.

Although Antioch tried to gain control of the Church of Cyprus, its independence was confirmed by a miraculous event, considered a major landmark in the history of the island: the discovery of the tomb of St. Barnabas at Salamis in 488. The Cypriot Archbishop Anthemios, so the story goes, had a visionary dream in which the location of the tomb was revealed. The archbishop found the body of the saint and with it a copy of the gospel of St. Matthew. Anthemios travelled to Constantinople to show the gospel to the Emperor Zeno, who viewed its discovery as a sign from God. Not only did he recognize the Church of Cyprus as autocephalous (equal to and independent of Constantinople), but he also extended three important privileges still enjoyed by today's

A proud minaret adorns Larnaca, while Byzantium lives on in the rich iconostasis at Kiti, opposite.

prelate: the right to hold a sceptre, to wear a purple mantle and to use red ink for his signatures.

The following two centuries were generally peaceful for Cyprus, since it was removed from the interminable wars that plagued the Byzantine empire.

Rise of Islam

In 647 Saracen Arabs invaded and devastated Cyprus. Constantia was destroyed, never to recover its past glories, as the island became a bone of contention between Christian Byzantium and Islam. For the next three centuries Cyprus changed hands at least eleven times, sometimes paying taxes simultaneously to the Byzantine emperor and the caliph, both of whom used the island as a military base. Arab incursions always meant slaughter, deportation and slavery of Cypriots.

The beleaguered coastal cities lost population as people retrenched into strongholds farther from the sea or repaired to new forts. But the Byzantines were recovering some of their old force; finally, in 965, Emperor Nicephoros Phocas ousted the Arabs and stopped the raiding.

For the next two centuries, Cyprus participated in the golden age of the empire, and a

Byzantine governor known as a *katapan* held sway. New towns were built on or near the sites of old, mainly ruined cities. Ammochostos (now Famagusta) succeeded Salamis. Lemesos (now Limassol) replaced the former Amathus, and Larnaca, the one-time Kition. Lefkosia (now Nicosia) was founded on a very ancient site called Ledra and became the island's principal city near the end of the 7th century. Many new churches and monasteries were put up and the art of fresco painting prospered. By the 12th century, Byzantine power began to fade away again, and Cyprus—owing to its strategic position—provided the crusaders with a staging place and stronghold.

Between 1184 and 1191, the Byzantine tyrant Isaac Comnenos ruled Cyprus. Then it was conquered by Richard I (the Lionheart) of England. Richard ceded the island to the Knights Templar and then to Guy de Lusignan, deposed King of Jerusalem, whose dynasty would succeed him for centuries to come.

Lusignans and Venetians

The new lords of Cyprus imposed a system of feudal rule, granting fiefs to their fellow crusaders and reducing most of the native Cypriots to serfdom. An archbishopric was created in Nicosia, and a papal bull of 1260 formalized the supremacy of the Roman Catholic church over the Orthodox (although in the end the Orthodox church survived persecution to become the dominant Christian force on Cyprus). When the crusaders lost Acre, their last foothold in the Holy Land, to the Egyptian Mamelukes in 1291, Christian refugees flooded into Cyprus. Fortress castles like St. Hilarion, Buffavento and Kantara reached completion, and work continued on some beautiful buildings in French Gothic style: Bellapais Abbey (near Kyrenia), St. Sophia, the cathedral of Nicosia, and Famagusta's St. Nicholas.

In the 14th century, the island gained importance as a centre for trade with the Middle East, accruing the profits of peace and commerce. A great rivalry grew up among Cyprus's merchants and the mercantile republics of Genoa and Venice for control of Cypriot trade in general and the port of Famagusta in particular—notorious for its luxuries and high living. The Lusignan kingdom reached its zenith when Peter I (reigned 1359–1369) won land on the Anatolian coast and led the last crusade against the Mamelukes, culminating in the sack of Alexandria.

However, Famagusta was in Genoese hands by 1373, and in 1426 Limassol and Larnaca were sacked by the Egyptian Mamelukes. In an effort to keep Egyptians from swarming over the whole island, the Cypriots agreed to pay a huge indemnity, swear an oath of allegiance and "donate" an annual tribute to the Egyptian sultan.

The last Lusignan king, James II, wrested Famagusta from the Genoese in 1473 and formed an alliance with Venice, taking as his queen a Venetian, Catherine Cornaro. Within two years of marriage, he died mysteriously and his baby son with him, leaving Catherine to rule alone. She abandoned the throne to the Venetian Republic in 1489, as the Ottoman Turks were extending their influence all over the Levant. At great expense to Cypriot taxpayers, the Venetians built heavy fortifications against the Turks. Meanwhile trade was declining due to the opening of new routes across the Atlantic and around the Cape of Good Hope. Venice could not hope to hold Cyprus forever, with the Turks in control of territory all around.

The long-dreaded invasion took place in 1570, and although Nicosia fell within about six weeks, Famagusta valiantly withstood the onslaught for nearly a year, capitulating at last in August, 1571. Most of the island's wealth had been depleted and many Cypriots had been killed.

Ottoman Turks Take Over

Venice formally renounced her claims to Cyprus in March, 1573, and the island became a destitute possession of the Ottoman empire. The Ottoman Turks exacted taxes and tribute money, but they left their conquered peoples a certain autonomy. In the case of Cyprus, Turkey recognized the Greek Orthodox Church and converted the Latin churches into mosques. This pleased the Cypriots, since their preferred religion had been outlawed by the Lusignans and Venetians.

The Turks also eliminated Western feudalism, freeing the serfs and allotting land to Turkish soldiers—but also to the Cypriots, who became largely self-governing agricultural free tenants. But in spite of these liberal policies, the rule of the sultan proved oppressive: local Turkish officials constantly dunned native Cypriots of all classes for tax tribute or bribe money and ignored the upkeep of civic properties such as roads, bridges and castles.

Famine and drought caused another kind of havoc on Cyprus, reducing the taxable population to 25,000 by 1641—down from 85,000 just 70 years before. Gradually, however, the Cypriots were coming into their own; by 1754 the sultan acknowledged the archbishop of the Orthodox church as head of the Church of Cyprus, which meant in effect that he was ethnarch—the leader of the Greek Cypriot nation.

During the years of mainland and island Greek unrest and rebellion against the Turks (1818–21), Cypriots, too, were chafing. But in 1821 the Turks nipped a Cypriot rising in the bud by executing the archbishop and several priests, as well as other citizens, including important officials. This inglorious episode served only to undermine Turkish authority.

An expansionist Russia and Great Britain meanwhile threatened the balance of power in the eastern Mediterranean, and with the Russian-Turkish war of 1828–29, the Ottoman empire was fast waning. Mehmet Ali of Egypt, Russia's ally, was poised to take Cyprus from Turkey when the British, fearing the Russian menace even more, sided with the Turks. In

exchange for British help, the Ottomans moderated their policies and initiated reforms. As a result, life changed for the better on Cyprus. The economy picked up, schooling was improved and Greek Cypriots gained greater influence in the administration of island affairs.

British Involvement

In an effort to protect Turkey against a belligerent Russia, Britain took over the administration of Cyprus in 1878, promising to pay the sultan in tribute any revenue over expenditure. This caused discomfiture both in Cyprus and in Great Britain.

For their part, Greek Cypriots generally welcomed the British, who—true to their usual form in colonial matters —instituted traditional administrative methods and legal procedures under a succession of high commissioners. They abolished abusive tax collection, reduced crime, improved schools, roads and water distribution. Although population, trade and agriculture grew considerably, prosperity did not meet high Cypriot expectations. Moreover, many islanders began to nourish a growing resentment against the British, owing to their seeming indifference to self-rule for Cyprus.

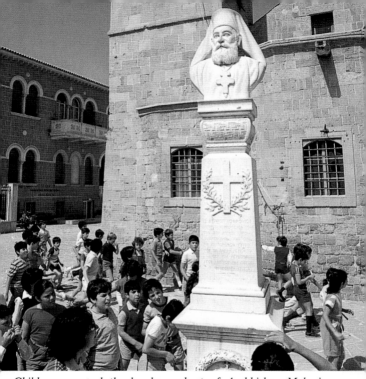

Children surround the handsome bust of Archbishop Makarios, by St. John's Cathedral, a well-known landmark of Nicosia.

At the outset of World War I, the British offered to turn over Cypriot administration to Greece if Greece would enter the war on the Allied side. But Greece remained neutral until 1917. When Turkey sided against Great Britain in 1914, the British formally annexed Cyprus. Turkey renounced all **23** claims to the island by terms of the Treaty of Lausanne (1923). Two years later Cyprus became a crown colony.

With Cypriot fervour for union with Greece *(enosis)* came stirrings of nationalism and a yearning for true independence. Following World War II, Cypriots rejected the British offer of a constitution.

Archbishop Makarios II organized a plebiscite that claimed a 96 per cent majority vote for *enosis*. Greece took up Cyprus's cause and put out inflammatory propaganda against Great Britain. As ethnarch or virtual ruler of Cyprus, Archbishop Makarios III was a fiery promoter of independence from Great Britain—fully applauded, of course, by Greece, where he had many friends in high places.

Wary of unstable conditions in Greece and unsure of how to treat Cypriot demands, Britain's Conservative government adopted a rather rigid stance in clinging to Cyprus, without proposing viable solutions. In 1955, isolated acts of violence erupted into an undeclared "war of independence". Finally the British administration invited Greece and Turkey to settle the trouble at a conference in London but negotiations foundered.

EOKA (National Organization of Freedom Fighters) activists, led by Georgios Grivas (code name, Dhigenis), a native Cypriot who had served as a colonel in the Greek army, systematically attacked and bombed British military personnel and installations from a hideout in the Troodos mountains. Nationalistic feelings were enthusiastically fanned by Archbishop Makarios and other religious leaders as the island was sporadically inflamed by violence. In retaliation, the British governor sent him into exile.

The "Cyprus question" finally went before the United Nations in 1957. Turkish Cypriots, alarmed by the prospect of *enosis,* had begun to clamour for partition, and violence on the island reached a new high. After many a false start and convoluted negotiations, the Treaty of Zurich (1959) declared the principle of an independent Cyprus with Greece, Turkey and Great Britain as guarantor powers, while granting Great Britain sovereign rights to military bases. Makarios signed the document—reluctantly—on behalf of Greek Cypriots, and Fazil Küchük as representative of Turkish Cypriots. On August 16, 1960, Cyprus achieved independence within the Commonwealth. Makarios became the first president and Küchük the first vice-president. Membership in the United Nations followed in 1961.

The constitution—which provided for a dual government of Greek and Turkish Cypriots—had proved a failure by 1963, as President Makarios, a champion of Cypriot unity, came to loggerheads with Vice-President Küchük, who wanted segregation of Greek and Turkish communities. This basic disagreement was to prove tragic.

In February of the following year, the United Nations sent a peace-keeping force to Cyprus. Through the years of instability that followed, Cyprus developed a vigorous tourist industry and the economy continued to grow. New elections in 1968 returned Makarios and Küchük to power. The Turks and Greeks on Cyprus viewed one another with increasing suspicion, although real violence did not surface until 1974.

Divided Island

In July 1974, the Greek military junta mounted a *coup d'état* to overthrow Makarios, with whom they violently disagreed. The Turks took swift action to "defend" Turkish Cypriots (who were not in much real danger), and sent in troops, who ravaged parts of the island. After nearly three weeks of fierce fighting, the Turks finally gained control of about 37 per cent of the territory, forcing some 200,000 Greek Cypriots into exile in the southern part of Cyprus and dispatching mainland Turkish soldiers and settlers to Kyrenia, Famagusta and other northern towns. By military force Turkey had precipitated the partition of Cyprus. A barrier went up to divide the country in two, and the United Nations acted as a peace-keeping force, with military police from various countries.

After the death of Archbishop Makarios in 1977, attempts to unite Cyprus burgeoned and fizzled periodically. Then, in November 1983, Turkish Cyprus unilaterally declared independence, which effectively and formally reinforced the existing partition.

Early in 1985, hopes for unity were raised prematurely when talks between Turkish and Greek Cypriots convened at the United Nations in New York. Agreement was not reached, but both sides appear willing to continue the search for a solution of the problems that have divided them for so long. **25**

CYPRUS

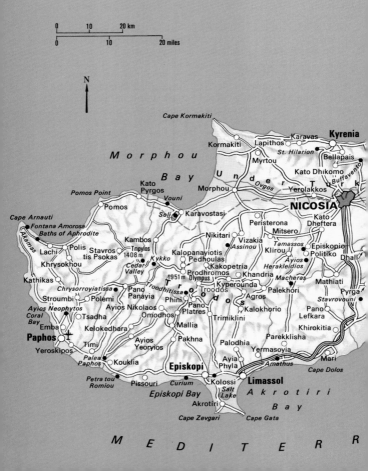

Cape Apostolos Andreas

Rizokarpaso

Cape Plakoti

Yialousa

Leonarisso   Korovia

Komi Kebir   Koma tou Yialou
Kantara
Akanthou   Ayios Theodhoros

Antiphonitis
Ayios
Amvrosios   Trikomo
Pentadaktylos
s   Lefkóniko   *F a m a g u s t a*
Marathovouno   Ayios Seryios

St. Barnabas   Salamis   *B a y*
Enkomi

Asha   **Famagusta**
Lysi
Athna   Dherinia
Athienou   *Protaras Beach*
Paralimni
Pyla   Avgorou   Sotira
radhippou   Ayia Napa
Dhekelia   Xylophagou
Larnaca   Cape Pyla   Cape Greco
Salt Hala
Lake Sultan Tekke
iti   *L a r n a c a*
Cape Kiti   *B a y*

A N   *S   E   A*

N   E   A   N

Where to Go

The Republic of Cyprus is small, allowing visitors to cover most of the tourist sights in a series of short trips from one or two bases*. But it's much more enjoyable to stay in several towns, savouring the atmosphere and surroundings to the fullest.

We therefore start with the capital and largest city, Nicosia, a must on any itinerary, moving on to the eastern part of the coast as enjoyed from beachside Larnaca. Next we visit Limassol, a large and growing tourist centre on the south coast. From there we continue westwards along the coast to beautiful Paphos and environs, with a leisurely stop inland in the Troodos mountain area—a cool weekend resort for residents of both Nicosia and Limassol.

The itinerary we propose is merely a suggestion, to be altered according to time available.

---

*Since November 1983, travel between Greek and Turkish-occupied Cyprus has been restricted. Permission to cross the border is granted only in exceptional circumstances. In this book, we concentrate mainly on the Greek-Cypriot part of the island, describing highlights of the north in the chapter "Northern Cyprus" (pp. 82–85).

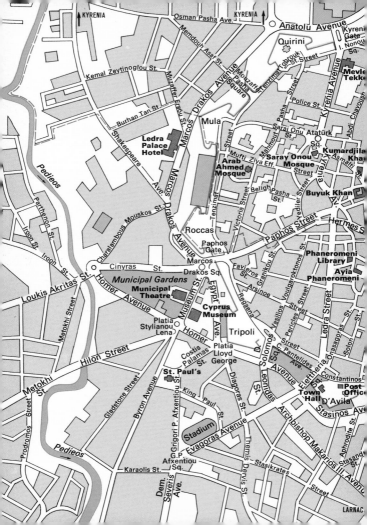

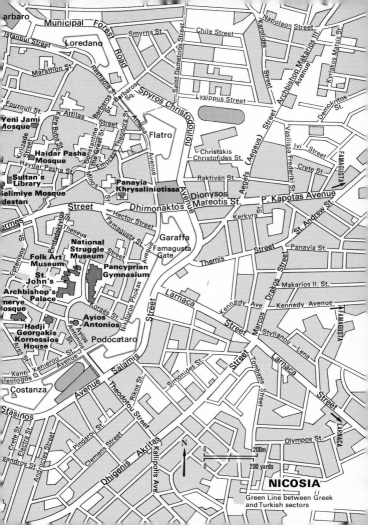

NICOSIA

Green Line between Greek
and Turkish sectors

Nicosia

This lively, bustling capital adorned with acres of green space is nevertheless a divided city, split by barbed-wire barriers into two sectors, Greek and Turkish. At least 75 per cent of Nicosia's 160,000 population live in the southern or Greek part of town.

Nicosia* (*Lefkosia* in Greek, *Lefkosha* in Turkish) is not only Cyprus's largest city, but its only inland metropolitan area, with excellent hotel, restaurant, shopping and entertainment possibilities—while for tourists, Nicosia makes a good base for sight-seeing excursions.

Nicosia's history goes back to Neolithic times. Situated near the ancient site of Ledra, today's city was founded in the 4th century B.C. by Lefkon, son of Ptolemy I. of Egypt. The origins of the name Lefkosia are still moot. It could have been inspired by Lefkon himself or by the word *lefki* ("poplar" in Greek). With the arrival of the Lusignans in the 12th century A.D., the city was

_____
*In our spelling of place names, we conform with Cypriot practice. However, the Greek phrases given in the practical information section, pages 106 to 126, follow our standard system of transcription, incorporating accent marks to facilitate pronunciation.

dubbed Nicosie (transformed by the British into Nicosia).

When coastal towns like Paphos and Salamis came under attack in the early 7th century A.D., the population shifted to the interior and Nicosia became chief city of the island. Under the Lusignans, Nicosia evolved into a splendid capital city. From the 12th to 15th centuries, Nicosia's golden age, castles, churches and monasteries in French Gothic style were constructed. Just prior to

Mouth-watering array of fresh produce tempts market visitors.

the Turkish invasion of 1570, Venetians built the massive defensive wall still standing.

When the Ottoman Turks took over after a six-week siege, 20,000 citizens lost their lives. Resistance to Ottoman rule flared up into outright rebellion in 1821, but the Turks suppressed the revolt. Nicosia suffered an outbreak of cholera in 1835 and a disastrous fire in 1857. And the heaviest fighting of the 1974 Turkish invasion took place here (some old bombed buildings are still deserted or serve as warehouses). But the buoyant city has survived all that to retain fascinating architectural reminders of past rulers, whether Lusignan, Venetian, Turkish or British. Since partition, scores of glossy new buildings have gone up—happily not high-rise.

Greek Quarter

The defensive wall built by the Venetians between 1567 and 1570 remains a prime feature of Nicosia. The unique shape of this wheel-like fortification provides a symbolic logo for the modern capital city and even for the Greek-Cypriot nation. Originally three main gates—Famagusta, Kyrenia and Paphos—pierced the ponderous, thick stone walls, nearly three miles in circumference. Nowadays Famagusta Gate (see p. 37) serves as a city cultural centre and some of the bastions shelter municipal offices, while certain sections of the moat have been trans-

The Archbishop's Palace, Nicosia, is a bright Venetian fantasy.

formed into public gardens, car parks and playgrounds.

Life within the walls revolves around **Eleftheria Square** (Liberty Square), where you'll find the Municipal Library, the Central Post Office and the Town Hall—this last a fanciful colonnaded structure of 1930, renovated in 1952. From the square, **Ledra Street** leads through the thriving old part of town, thronged with shoppers for popularly priced goods. You'll want to explore the crowded alleyways and tiny

streets lined with shops, cafés and food stands exuding exotic odours, especially late in the day when the air is cooler.

Opened in 1984, the revived **Popular Neighbourhood** *(Laiki Yitonia)* recreates the atmosphere of old Nicosia. Buildings in traditional style—some restored, others specially constructed—house quaint boutiques, tavernas, flats and artisans' galleries (you can watch the craftsmen while they work), as well as an office of the Cyprus Tourism Organization.

To glimpse more of history's landmarks, stay within the inner city. Religious edifices include the **Ayia Phaneromeni**

church in Phaneromeni Street, erected in 1872 with stones remaining from an old castle and monastery. The church is the burial place of Nicosia's archbishop and bishops slain by the Turks in the rebellion of 1821. The adjacent library shelters an interesting collection of old icons. Omerye Mosque with its small minaret (now closed) began life as an Augustinian monastery.

At 18 Patriarch Gregorios Street, the house of Hadjigeorgakis Kornessios, **Konak Mansion,** is a beautiful 18th-century structure with Gothic arches and doorway and overhanging, closed balcony. Restored to its original splendour, the interior preserves a painted ceiling, decorated stairway and original furnishings. It was built by a rich Cypriot who served as *dragoman* (an agent of the Turkish sultan) from 1779 to 1809.

The **Archbishop's Palace** (closed to visitors) lies nearby in Zenon of Kition Street. This stunning modern pastiche of Venetian architecture was begun in 1956. Some call it vulgar; others are impressed. However, the opulence of the public rooms does not extend to the former bedroom of Archbishop Makarios III. With a simple chest and iron bed, the room makes a humble resting place for the archbishop's heart.

Housed in a wing of the Archbishop's Palace, the Makarios Cultural Centre comprises galleries of European and Greek art, as well as the superb **Byzantine Museum**, opened in 1978. It boasts good presentation and lighting and—most important—well-regulated air and humidity conditions for preservation of a unique collection of icons. Many of the works on display were saved from insalubrious conditions in neglected churches or monasteries. Painted between the 9th and 18th centuries, the icons represent the full gamut of Byzantine art on Cyprus. From its 12th-century zenith comes the figure of *Christ* clothed in purple, his hand raised in blessing; and the *Virgin of Arakas,* a solemn interpretation of the mother and child theme.

Upstairs hangs a prodigious array of European paintings from the 16th to 19th centuries. In spite of vast wall coverage, this must be termed largely a collection of minor works by little-known artists. More interesting are the pictures of Greek themes: Delacroix's *After the Massacre,* an impassioned portrayal of the massacre of Chios, and *The Sad News in 1897* by Rallis, inspired by the war between Greece and Turkey that year.

Right next door, you can't miss **St. John's** *(Ayios Ioannis),* the Orthodox cathedral of Nicosia. Built in 1665 on the site of a former Benedictine Abbey, the simple, vaulted construction in golden stone emulates Late Gothic style. A series of 18th-century **fresco paintings** decorates the interior. Have a look at the scenes depicting big moments in religion for Cyprus: St. Paul and St. Barnabas bringing Christianity to the island in A.D. 45; the miraculous dream of Archbishop

Anthemios; the discovery of St. Barnabas's tomb; and the bestowing of privileges on the Archbishop of Cyprus in A.D. 488 by Emperor Zeno (see p. 18).

The pleasant Gothic-arcaded monastery building adjacent (the Old Archbishopric) was renovated in the early 1960s as the premises of the **Folk Art Museum,** noted for its intriguing exhibits. You'll see wooden water wheels, old looms (one ostensibly in use), pottery, elaborately carved and painted bridal chests, lace and embroidered costumes. Notice especially the hand-woven and embroidered cotton outfits for women *(saghies),* the men's waistcoats or vests *(zimbounia)* and baggy pants *(vraka),* as well as some appealing naïve paintings on wood by an artist named Kashalos, a patriot who died (some say of a broken heart) shortly after the Turkish invasion of 1974. His meticulous works take as their subject traditional Cypriot ceremonies and scenes.

Just a few steps away, the **National Struggle Museum** contains weapons, documents and photographs pertaining to the EOKA rebellion against British rule in the 1950s. If you're interested in the recent history of Cyprus, you'll find much of import here.

Cypriots have converted a good number of their historical monuments to new uses. A case in point is the **Famagusta Gate and Cultural Centre,** a few minutes' walk to the northeast. The Venetian portal of 1567, once the main gate of old Nicosia, provides a venue for contemporary art exhibitions, while the beautifully restored stone barrel vaults and thick walls of the gate are in themselves an impressive attraction. During the annual Nicosia arts festival, an outdoor theatre for concerts and plays is set up nearby, on the site of an old Turkish warehouse.

Of course, there's lots to see and do outside the old walls in sprawling Nicosia. For sophisticated shopping, dining and nightlife, you'll want to visit Evagoras and Archbishop Makarios avenues, south of Eleftheria Square.

Just west of Paphos Gate in Museum Street—not far from the main shopping thoroughfares—stands the **Cyprus Museum,** a treasure-trove of major Cypriot archaeological and art works.

Some of the most interesting pieces in the collection come from the Bronze Age (2,300–1,050 B.C.): red-polished and white-painted pottery, stylized terracotta figurines, a clay **37**

model of a sacred enclosure, Mycenaean *kraters* (drinking cups)—one interestingly adorned with bulls, trees, chariots. The magisterial bronze *Horned God* (13th century B.C.), a statue nearly two feet high, comes from the sanctuary at Enkomi; and the blue faïence rhyton or drinking vessel (12th century B.C.) was found at Kition. It stands out for its lively painted decoration of a bull hunt.

You can't miss the huge showcase displaying terracotta votive statues and figurines of the 7th and 6th centuries B.C. from Ayia Irini in north-west Cyprus. Excavated by the Swedish-Cypriot expedition of 1929, this overwhelming group comprises mainly warriors, minotaurs and charioteers—some life-size—in an impressive display of "male chauvinism": out of 2,000 figures only two female statuettes were found. Notice, too, the conical stone from Palea Paphos associated with Aphrodite worship (see p. 76).

The museum contains some beautiful archaic and classical **statues.** The most striking of them may well be the limestone *Head of a Woman from Arsos* (early 3rd century B.C.)—an outstanding portrait with a face both sensual and wise. Just as compelling, the small, marble *Aphrodite from Soli* (1st century B.C.) has a cool, classical allure. The towering bronze statue of the Roman Emperor Septimus Severus (A.D. 193–211) is an outstanding work of Roman-Cypriot art; the nude emperor strikes a tense pose that might be interpreted as oratorical.

A fascinating group of reconstructed tombs and their original contents span the centuries from the 3rd millennium to around 400 B.C. Also of special interest are gold objects excavated from tombs at Palea Paphos, dating from the 11th to 8th centuries B.C.

Across the street from this ever-growing museum are the Municipal Theatre (1967) and the welcoming, shady **Municipal Gardens**.

Cyprus's modern **Handicrafts Centre** in Athalassa Avenue lies south of the town centre. It was founded in 1980 to provide refugees from northern Cyprus with a source of income. You can watch craftsmen and women ply their trades from 7.30 a.m. to 2 p.m. Around the quiet courtyard are rooms for embroidery, weaving, wood-carving, pottery, leather-tooling and so on. You don't have to buy anything at the gift shop, but you might find some irresistible souvenirs. **39**

Turkish Quarter*

As in the Greek quarter, most of the tourist sights lie within the walled city. From Kyrenia Gate, follow the avenue of the same name to **Mevlevi Tekke**, once a monastery inhabited by members of the whirling dervishes sect, outlawed in 1925. The 17th-century building with its several domes now houses a **Museum of Arts and Crafts** whose exhibits include embroidery, costumes, musical instruments and dolls in Turkish-Cypriot costumes. The mausoleum nearby contains 16 tombs of the leaders of the Mevlevi sect, including that of the last, Selim Debe, who died in 1954.

Brownstone government office buildings rim **Atatürk Square**, hub of the Turkish quarter. Here stands the post office and a granite column probably brought from Salamis by the Venetians. The Turks removed it when they conquered Cyprus in 1570, and it was re-erected in 1915. Unfortunately the St. Mark's lion once crowning it disappeared, and the copper globe you see is a recent addition.

From Atatürk Square, Asmalti Street leads past a couple of old Turkish **inns** with picturesque courtyards and verandahs: Kumardjilar Khan (now restored) and Buyuk Khan. In the 18th century the Turks built these *khans* or *hans* as hospices for visiting foreigners. A main door gave onto a courtyard surrounded by rooms. Although the main door was bolted, a smaller door within it, called the "eye of the needle", was left open for travellers—so that camels, carts and other conveyances could not enter.

Further down the street you come to a highlight of northern Nicosia, the Cathedral of Santa Sophia, now known as **Selimiye Mosque**. In spite of the somewhat incongruous minarets thrusting skywards, this is one of the finest examples of French Gothic architecture in Cyprus. The cathedral was begun in 1209 under the first Latin archbishop, Thierry, reaching completion in the 14th century. Here the Lusignan princes were crowned kings of Cyprus, and here Christian worship took place—until the Turks turned the church into a mosque following the 1570 conquest. Note the western façade and its porch with three portals surmounted by a rose

*At the time of going to press, permission to enter the Turkish quarter could be obtained only in exceptional circumstances. Inquire locally, as the situation may have changed.

window; with moulded ogival arches and carved figures of saints, royalty and clergy, this could be a cathedral transported straight from France.

The **Bedestan** or old market next door dates from the 12th to the 14th centuries, when it was constructed as the Church of St. Nicholas-of-the-English. The Turks converted the church into a covered market—today disused. But you can still admire the carved Gothic doors, the family crests and religious sculptures above the main portal, the barrel-shaped roof, three apses and dome. In the crumbling interior are some wall paintings, notably one of St. Andrew (12th century).

Also near the cathedral, the **Sultan's Library** preserves important books in Turkish, Arabic and Persian.

Excursions

The following sights lie within a 30-mile radius of Nicosia and can easily be visited from the capital.

The ancient city-kingdom of **Tamassos** (near Politiko village) was famed for its copper mines. Excavations of the once-rich city were begun in the late 19th century, when the 6th-century B.C. **tombs** were uncovered; looted in antiquity, they contained no treasure, apart from a silver dish with a horse's head, now in the Cyprus Museum in Nicosia. But the structures themselves are interesting for their carved decoration. Since 1971 German archaeological teams have been at work on the Tamassos site, excavating the temple of Aphrodite and part of a defensive wall.

A couple of miles south-west of Tamassos at POLITIKO village is the **Monastery of Ayios Herakleidios,** a peaceful country retreat now inhabited by nuns, who keep up the gardens and sell honey, marzipan and other sweets. The monastery was destroyed and restored several times; the structure you see today was built by Archbishop Chrysanthos in the 18th century. The body of the saint for whom the monastery is named reposes in a crypt of the domed church. Guide to St. Paul and St. Barnabas on their journey around Cyprus in A.D. 45, St. Herakleidios went on to become first bishop of Tamassos. He also died a martyr to the faith —killed by pagans who burned him alive. A gold reliquary encrusted with jewels contains the saint's skull and a hand bone.

The **Monastery of Macheras** (south-west of Ayios Herakleidios) lies at an impressive height of 2,900 feet above the 41 sea in a landscape of great beauty. The monastery was founded in the 12th century, but none of the old buildings survived a devastating fire in 1892. *Machera* means "knife" in Greek, a name that comes either from the cold, cutting winds that blow through in winter or from a knife that was discovered in a cave, along with a miracle-working icon of the Virgin Mary.

During the EOKA rebellion of the 1950s Gregoris Afxentiou, second in command of guerilla troops, put up a ten-hour battle in the area. On March 3, 1957, he was finally burned alive not far from the monastery in his forest hideout.

West from Nicosia, follow signs after PERISTERONA (about 19 miles from Nicosia) for **Assinou Church**—also called Church of Panayia Phorbiatissa —known for its charm and outstanding Byzantine frescoes. Stop at the little village of NIKI-TARI to pick up the priest and keeper of the keys, and then drive with him to Assinou.

The small church is an unpretentious little masterpiece of ochre stone. The barrel-vaulted interior dates from the early 12th century, though it was later reinforced (the domed narthex is from the late 12th century). The frescoes consti-

tute a picture gallery of Byzantine art from the 12th to 16th centuries. You'll see a *Pantokrator* (Christ in Majesty) of 1333 in the narthex dome; the son of God forms a ring with his thumb and fourth finger in the Orthodox gesture of blessing. The *Last Judgement* shows the blessed and damned: as usual, the heavenward-headed blessed ones look a dreary lot, while the damned are a colourful group complete with a snake, fire and dramatic expressions

of agony. The nave and bays of the church display the *Washing of the Feet,* the *Raising of Lazarus,* the *Crucifixion* and *Entombment,* among other scenes. If the priest forgets to light the church, remind him with a smile and thank him with some money when you return to the village.

Larnaca

A lively influx of refugees, tourists and others are fast swelling the basic population of 28,000. Seaside seekers find lots to attract them, and for art lovers the Pierides collection and St. Lazarus Church are major magnets.

Most of northern Larnaca is built on the site of the ancient city-kingdom of Kition (Kittim to the Turks). Legend attributes its founding to Kittim, a

Flowers galore against white walls—Cyprus in a nutshell.

grandson of Noah, whose name appears in the Bible. Recent excavations have unearthed evidence of occupation as far back as the 2nd millennium B.C., making this the oldest still-inhabited city of Cyprus. Mycenaeans originally settled Larnaca, but Phoenicians took over for several centuries from the 9th century B.C., making the city-kingdom theirs.

An ally of Persia, ancient Kition was gradually put down by the Greco-Persian wars (5th century B.C.). The Greek general, Kimon of Athens, lay siege to the city in 449 B.C., but it did not fall. Finally, in 312 B.C., the Phoenician kingship came to an end. One illustrious citizen of that time was the philosopher Zeno (or Zenon), founder of the Stoic school in Athens, who was born in Kition in 336 B.C.

A fire in 280 B.C. inflicted further damage on the city in decline. Meanwhile, a new centre was developing at the harbour, Scala—later called by the name Salines, in reference to the salt lake nearby. Under the Lusignans, the town (now known as Larnaca) grew in importance, especially as a commercial and shipping centre.

Larnaca continued to flourish during the Turkish occupation, when a number of foreign consulates were set up here. In the last century, many administrative and business offices moved to Famagusta, resulting in a slump; but today, due to the new prestige of the airport and port—the principal gateways to the Republic of Cyprus —Larnaca is on the rise again.

To begin any visit, start along seafront **Athens Street**, also named Phinikoudhes Boulevard (Palm Tree Boulevard) after its very tall but rather drab specimens. From the pleasure-boat port, or marina, down the wide, sandy beach, it's a colourful promenade past food stands, cafés and tavernas.

Walking south you reach the **Turkish Fort** (1625), now a museum. Some objects from Kition and the Hala Sultan Tekke are on display, but most exhibits are photographs of local archaeological finds. A staircase leads up the defensive wall to a good harbour view.

A couple of streets inland is the town's most prominent old structure, the **Church of St. Lazarus** (Ayios Lazaros). Lazarus, the patron saint of Larnaca, supposedly sailed into port after his famous resurrection at Bethany in Palestine, became bishop of Kition, died, and was buried here. In 890 his tomb was found, but most of the relics were removed.

Raised in the 9th century over the Lazarus tomb, the church was rebuilt several times. When you enter through the south door under the 19th-century three-tiered "Gothic" campanile, you find an impressive, if somewhat eclectic sight of three aisles in Romanesque and early Gothic style, three Byzantine domes on pendentives and a dazzling array of icons, silver furnishings and carved woodwork. If you visit late in the day, you'll see the church worthies collecting offerings from big boxes—emptying them into buckets in incredible volume.

On the iconostasis hang many scenes of the life of Christ, at least two representations of Lazarus on his way out of the tomb (in one of them a bystander can't help holding his nose) and an icon of the *Virgin and Child*. Visitors usually go down to the crypt to see St. Lazarus's tomb.

A small English cemetery alongside the church contains many marked graves of merchants, seamen and consuls dating from the 17th to 19th centuries.

A few steps inland from the marina stands the tourist office in its warmly flowered setting. Around the corner in Zenon Kitieos Street you'll see the **Pierides Museum**—an archaeological collection installed in the old Pierides family home, a pretty white building with a verandah. The Swedish honorary consul, Demetrios Pierides (1811–1895), amassed the core of the collection, which was augmented by several generations of family members.

The thousands of objects displayed here cover Cypriot history from Neolithic to Byzantine times. You'll see sculpted pottery in lively bird shapes, expressive statuettes (notice a fat little terracotta figure, screaming, from the Chalcolithic era) and idols of the love-goddess Astarte type. Hundreds of figurines and glazed ceramic objects complete this collection, which also includes an interesting selection of Roman glass dated 200 B.C. to A.D. 300. Some Pierides family relics and furnishings are displayed as well.

To the north-west, in a garden fronted by a mosaic pavement, the **District Museum** (Kilkis and Kimon streets) offers an eclectic collection of sculpture and objects from Neolithic through medieval times. But the basis of the collection is very early finds from Kition and other sites in the Larnaca district—ornaments, vases, lamps, tools and mirrors.

Uphill, between the District Museum and Arkhiepiskopos Kyprianos Avenue, lies the Kition Acropolis, one of the oldest parts of the city. Rebuilt by the Phoenicians in the 9th century B.C., Kition remained a principal Phoenician city-kingdom until 312 B.C. The site is mainly of interest to experts. In the early 1960s, in an **excavation** just to the north of the Acropolis, a treasure-trove of Mycenean and Egyptian objects was discovered, showing that the area was occupied as far back as the 13th century B.C. The pieces have been dispersed to various museums.

West of Larnaca
About 3 miles from town, in the direction of Larnaca airport, the **Salt Lake** extends over an area of some 2½ square miles. Situated 10 feet below sea level, it's impressive when seen covered with water in the spring, or when salt is being collected at the end of July—a backbreaking task. In autumn and winter, thousands of migratory flamingoes flock by in a colourful cloud of pink, as they do at Akrotiri near Limassol.

Hala Sultan Tekke, a Muslim shrine, looks like a mirage in the dry summer season—thrusting its minaret through

An oasis in a desert of salt flats: Hala Sultan Tekke Shrine.

greenery over the blinding white salt flats. An important Muslim pilgrimage place, the shrine purportedly contains the remains of the Prophet Mohammed's maternal aunt, Umm Haram (Foster Mother), known as Hala Sultan in Turkish. According to Muslim tradition, Umm Haram came to Cyprus with a party of Arab invaders

in 647 A.D. She fell from her mule near the Salt Lake, broke her neck and was buried here. The Turks built the mosque in her honour in 1816.

To enter, you leave your shoes at the door. The outer room has brightly painted octagonal columns and there is a women's gallery to the right. In the inner sanctuary, the guardian points out the trilithon structure above Umm Haram's grave—two enormous stones about 15 feet high, covered with a meteorite that is said to have come from Mecca. A legend relates that it hovered in the air by itself here for centuries.

A couple of miles further west is the village of KITI. Its famous church, **Panayia Angeloktistos** (Church of the Blessed Virgin Built by Angels), stands just north of the main crossroad. Domed and in golden stone, the present 11th-century edifice replaced a much earlier structure. At the entrance is **47** the 14th-century chapel belonging to a rich medieval family, the Gibelets. But the outstanding feature of the church is the splendid early Byzantine **mosaic** in the apse (all that remains of the original church) —considered to be the finest in Cyprus. Shown standing, the Virgin Mary holds the Christ Child, flanked by the archangels Michael and Gabriel. The gold background, elaborate ornamentation and forward-moving pose of the Virgin are reminiscent of the famous mosaic of Empress Theodora at Ravenna, Italy. Both mosaics were created in the same period, the 6th to 7th centuries.

At some 2,400 feet high, **Lefkara** (32 miles from Larnaca) actually comprises two villages, Pano Lefkara and Kato Lefkara, which occupy a picturesque site in the foothills of the Troodos mountains. The name Lefkara is synonymous with drawn embroidery *(lefkaritika),* the traditional cottage industry that has brought the village fame for over five centuries. Widely and wrongly known as lace, *lefkaritika* is linen openwork stitched with intricate geometric patterns. When Leonardo da Vinci visited Cyprus in 1481, he apparently was so taken with the needlework of Lefkara that he

bought yards of it for the altar of Milan Cathedral.

Women still work in narrow streets and courtyards, patiently turning out embroidered articles. Most of them sell their work to one of four major companies in Lefkara, so you can't exactly pluck a doily from the hands of the maker. But *lefkaritika* is readily available in shops here and all over Cyprus.

Just south is KHIROKITIA, a small village known mainly for its **Neolithic ruins.** One of the oldest sites in Cyprus, dating from 5,800 B.C., it was discovered in 1934 by Porfyrios Dikeos, then director of the Cyprus Museum. After a climb up some steep steps—on the other side of a bridge across from today's town—visitors reach the most interesting of four areas. You'll see a main street and the stone foundations of beehive-shaped houses *(tholos).* Made of clay or mud bricks, the dwellings were built in successive layers; when a structure fell down, a new one was put up to take its place. The dead were buried right in the cellar, so to speak: 26 skeletons were found in the ruins of one house. Among thousands of artefacts uncovered, many of interest (tools, idols, beads) are exhibited in Nicosia's Cyprus Museum.

The chores of monastery life leave no time to enjoy Cape Greco.

Returning to Larnaca, you may want to make a detour north to **Stravrovouni** (Mountain of the Cross), a monastery situated on top of a spectacular peak. Difficult of access, the monastery can only be reached via a steep, unpaved road. Purportedly founded in A.D. 327 by St. Helena, mother of the Emperor Constantine, the monastery as it exists today dates back to the 17th century. Women may visit on Sundays only, though men are welcome to stay overnight any day of the week.

East of Larnaca

Since Famagusta lies in the Turkish-occupied area, **Paralimni** is about as far east as you can go. This small town has come into its own as a sea resort since Famagusta was taken over by the Turks. The Paralimni area, along with Cape Greco *(Cavo Greco),* is known for its luminous light and hideaway coves, the beaches of Protaras and Fig Tree Bay, as well as the special Cypriot cuisine of some of the tiny villages. Both Greek poet George Seferis and French poet Arthur Rimbaud lived in this part of Cyprus and extolled its beauties in verse.

Going south around Cape Greco, with some splendid views of the sea (in spite of several large and intrusive radio antennae), you'll reach **Ayia Napa,** another sea resort popular since the closing-off of Famagusta. In spite of the spate of water-skiers, windsurfers and new development, Ayia Napa town has preserved much of its old fishing-village charm.

Here stands the **Monastery of Ayia Napa** (Our Lady of the Forest), built by Venetians sometime before the Turks came in 1570 and quite well preserved behind formidable stone walls. Originally a nunnery surrounded by conifers, today Ayia Napa occupies a rather barren-looking spot.

The charm of the monastery lies mainly in its peaceful Gothic-style cloister and an interior courtyard with a charming octagonal marble fountain surmounted by a cupola on four pillars. Carved out of the rock, the church lies partially underground; from the small chapel to the east you can descend steps to an ancient sycamore tree six centuries old, from where you have a great view down to the sea. In a modern building near the church the Ecumenical Conference of the World Council of Churches convenes.

Limassol

Local wags and boosters dub Limassol "Little Paris of Cyprus" for its gaiety, nightlife and wine interest. But there the resemblance ends, for this seaside boom-town is more like a small Miami Beach. The port resort ranks as Cyprus's second largest city (after Nicosia), and it bristles with all the attendant high-rise hotels and dwellings. From 80,000 in 1974 the population has swelled to nearly 110,000 today, mainly due to refugees from the Turkish invasion, plus additional settlers from Lebanon and the Near East.

Limassol boasts miles of sandy beach, especially in the eastern suburban area—with plenty of bright lights, little boutiques and snack bars by the road to give it a slightly raffish, honky-tonk air. But its main claim to fame is as Cyprus's major wine and spirits production and sales centre. Corks pop merrily during the September wine festival, when the local park turns into a free-wheeling open-air wine bar, as the various wineries offer free samples of their wares.

The Limassol urban area was apparently occupied by small settlements from 2,000 B.C. onwards. But the town itself was of little importance before the Christian era and the time of the crusades, around the 12th century. The main centres of antiquity had been the city-kingdoms of Amathus to the east, now just a heap of ancient rocks, and Curium (Kourion) to the west, still a place of interest to tourists. Hence, the probable origin of the name Limassol, conjectured to be a corruption of Nemesos, Greek for "in between" (the two ancient centres), which later became Lemesos and then Limassol.

The town's historical renown is largely due to Richard I (the Lionheart) of England, whose fiancée Berengaria was shipwrecked and blown ashore five miles away at Amathus en route to Jerusalem on the Third Crusade in 1191. The reigning ruler, Isaac Comnenos, welcomed the party with a show of arms and threats. So Richard and his troops came to the rescue, dispatching the incumbents in short order. The English overran the island but soon sold it—first to the Knights Templar (who settled in Limassol) and then to the Lusignans (see p. 20). The Knights of St. John made Limassol their

Hard to choose? Looking round shopping possibilities in Limassol.

headquarters for a time after 1291, and the town flourished as never before.

But Limassol's fortunes wavered as it swayed between the Venetians and the Turks. By the beginning of the 19th century, repeated invasions and earthquakes had reduced the once-proud city to a village. Development of the wine industry under the British brought new life to Limassol. Then came its astonishing rise as a resort.

City Sights

The main tourist attraction—and the only one to survive all those devastating earthquakes more or less intact—is the **castle,** just a few steps inland from the old port and customs house. The imposing stone fortification dates from the 13th century. Both the Lusignans and Venetians strengthened this ancient redoubt, which served the Turks as well after their conquest of Cyprus in 1571. In a pleasant tropical-greenery setting, it is surrounded by narrow lanes lined with artisans shops, where the speciality is metalware (copper and tin), and where the craftsmen are bemused rather than amused by tourists (although they're perfectly amenable).

The castle lies empty, except for the Great Hall, the Gothic chamber on the right as you enter. Converted for use as a church and then a prison, the hall has been restored to its original appearance. The prison seems a rather cosy-looking place now, with eight cells in pristine white limestone. Climb to the rooftop for a good view of the harbour.

Walking through the narrow, crowded shopping lanes radiating from Andreou and Anexartisias streets is an amusing way to see "old Limassol", and you might just find a bargain or two.

The small, modern **Limassol Museum** in Byron Street behind the Public Gardens contains some fascinating archaeological treasures. From shards and tools of Neolithic and Chalcolithic vintage, you'll progress through ceramics of the Bronze and Iron ages, with plenty of pottery right up through the Greco-Roman period (plus coins, rings and other artefacts).

Don't miss the display of jewellery from various periods and the expressive terracotta figurines; one fat lady with a basket looks like a friendly old-fashioned washerwoman, while bulls and outsize dogs complete the amusing statuette scene. There's a beautiful head of Aphrodite from nearby Curium; a headless statue of a youth holding a bird (7th–6th century B.C.); some funerary steles; and a massive statue of the Egyptian god Bes—indeed an ugly fellow—found on the site of ancient Amathus in 1978.

Graced with tall eucalyptus and palm trees, the **Zoological Gardens** make a cool retreat, except during the September wine festival when Bacchic revelries take over. Local attractions in the way of fauna include the wary little Cypriot fox and the tiny moufflon, a kind of sheep with spiralling horns.

As wine-making is not only an industry but a tourist attraction as well, you'll find a visit to a **winery** both instructive and fun. On the outskirts of town, the top houses—Keo, Sodap and Etko—all offer short tours of their plant. You'll see how Cypriot wines, beers and spirits are made and bottled, and you'll have a chance to taste. Tours usually begin around 10 a.m.

Excursions

Having exhausted the possibilities in town, most Limassol sightseers look farther afield. Eastwards near the main new hotels and vast beaches are the ruins of Amathus, though the old stones here make little sense to all but experts. It's more interesting to take the westward route to Petra tou Romiou, a mere 29 miles from Limassol. If you have a minimum of time, choose the direct road via Kolossi Castle; otherwise take the long way round the Akrotiri Peninsula, or combine the two, going one way, coming back the other.

A region of orange groves and vineyards, the **Akrotiri Peninsula** is famed for its salt flats and the stretch of sandy beach called Lady's Mile, named after a British colonel's mare who had her daily workout here. The **salt lake** is a good place for viewing migratory flamingoes, when the colourful pink birds pass through from October to March. Not far to the south-east (after AKROTIRI village), a tiny road leads to **St. Nicholas of the Cats Monastery** —a rambling Gothic ruin. The name derives from the fact that the monks of St. Nicholas supposedly trained cats to track down and kill poisonous snakes, the scourge of the region in the late Middle Ages.

On the west side of the peninsula, 7 miles from Limassol, **Kolossi Castle** is an impressive 15th-century keep, thrusting up from softly rolling countryside. The fortification was built **55**

Kolossi Castle is not far from the beautiful mosaics of Curium.

by the Knights of St. John of Jerusalem to replace an earlier tower erected by the order when it first took possession of the site in the 13th century. From Kolossi, the Knights administered vast sugar-cane estates and extensive vineyards. They derived their wealth from the production of sugar and sweet red Commandaria, Cyprus's famous dessert wine. (The name refers to the knights' headquarters or *commanderie,* established by the Knights of St. John at Kolossi.)

A stone stairway leads across the moat to the entrance. As you go into the stark interior, notice the fleur-de-lys coat of arms above the east side entry, identified with Louis de Magnac, the Lusignan nobleman who as Grand Commander of the Order of St. John oversaw construction of the castle. Of the vast rooms (the walls are ten feet thick), the one with a huge fireplace was apparently the kitchen. Visitors in good shape can take the narrow and steep spiral staircase to the roof with its battlements for good views.

Outside are traces of an ancient aqueduct. The main outbuilding is a handsome stone Gothic structure that was once used as a sugar refinery.

The main interest of the nearby village of EPISKOPI is the small Curium Museum, put together in the 1930s by an American archaeologist who assembled objects from nearby Curium and the Temple of Apollo—terracotta vases and figurines, limestone heads, a Roman lion fountain.

Curium (or Kourion) is a major Cypriot attraction just outside Episkopi (about 10 miles from Limassol). Although Herodotus wrote that Curium was founded around 1,200 B.C. by Greek immigrants from Argos in the Peloponnese, archaeologists have revealed earlier settlements, perhaps from the period of Mycenaean expansion in the 14th century B.C. There are two main areas to visit: the ancient town centre, site of the basilica and the fascinating Roman

theatre, and the outlying stadium and temple of Apollo Hylates.

One of the principal city-kingdoms of Cyprus, Curium was wealthy and important, especially during Roman times. When the American honorary consul-general, Luigi di Cesnola, ordered excavations begun here in 1876, a vast treasure of gold and silver jewellery was discovered, along with other valuable objects. The so-called Curium treasure was subse- **57** quently sold to New York's Metropolitan Museum of Art—creating a furor in Cyprus. In recent years, many interesting discoveries have been made—but no more gold treasure has come to light.

Turning into the old town centre of Curium from the main road, you'll find the sweeping **view** of Episkopi Bay and surroundings from the 30-foot-high bluff breathtaking. Before reaching the tourist pavilion (there's a restaurant here, operated by the Cyprus Tourism Organization) you'll see fenced-in ruins of a colonnaded portico, with a mosaic depicting Achilles disguised as a woman, inadvertently revealing his true identity to Odysseus. The House of the Gladiators nearby takes its name from a mosaic showing gladiators engaged in combat.

After the main entrance gate (where guide maps of the site are on sale), you come to the sparse remains of the early Christian **basilica** (c. 400) on the cliff side of the road. The view of the deep blue sea from here is majestic. Most of the excavation work was sponsored by the Dumbarton Oaks Center for Byzantine Studies in Washington D.C. Among the ruins of the one-time cathedral of Curium you'll see dozens of columns and capitals. Just adjacent is all that is left of the Bishop's Palace and the baptistery, with baptismal basin. Much of Curium was destroyed during earthquakes in 332 and 342, which also levelled most of Limassol; however, Curium was not abandoned until the mid-7th century A.D.

The restored **Roman theatre** dating from about A.D. 50 to 175 occupies a spectacular sloping site on the edge of the bluff. Visitors approach this awesome semi-circular structure from the top and can enjoy a great view and appreciate the architecture without having to climb down the steep steps to the orchestra area. Designed to seat 3,500 spectators, the theatre again serves as a venue for performances in the open air.

Just a bit further on are the remains of the **Villa of Eustolios**, a Roman mansion dating from the early 5th century A.D. The owner was obviously a rich aesthete, judging from the mosaic floors ornamented with stylized bird and fish motifs. The inscriptions, which have been partially effaced, relate to the villa's owner, to the patron deity of Curium (Apollo) and to Christ. The villa was later opened to the public as a bath house. Up a few steps are the **baths**. The

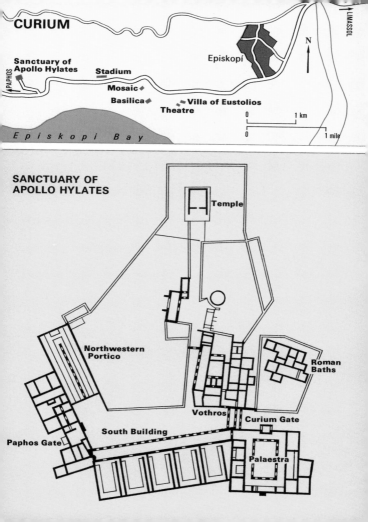

central room preserves some excellent **mosaics,** including one of a partridge and another of Ktisis, a female deity signifying creation. She holds an object that could have been a measuring rod. (It corresponds in length to one Roman foot.)

You have to go over to the main road and continue west half a mile to reach the U-shaped stadium, once the scene of sports competition, now reconstructed in part. West again (not far off the main road) lies the **Sanctuary of Apollo** or Apollo Hylates (God of the Woodland), situated in a rather scruffy pine grove. The Apollo cult was celebrated here from the 8th century B.C., but most of the present structures were put up around A.D. 100, only to be thrown down by earthquakes in the 4th century.

Most visitors approach this sacred place from the west, via **Paphos Gate.** The pilgrims of old probably found shelter in the buildings on either side. Both buildings may also have been used as storehouses for a never-ending stream of votive offerings. The surplus found its way into a pit called the *vothros,* which was full of terracotta figures when archaeologists uncovered it. A walk leads north from the Doric-porticoed building, past the *vothros,* to the surprisingly modest **Temple of Apollo,** heralded by a monumental flight of stairs. The portico of the temple, it seems, is where worship actually took place. A kind of ceremonial rampway links the temple to the area where animals were sacrificed. The buildings nearby may have been the priest's house and treasury.

If you leave the sanctuary by Curium Gate, you'll pass the remains of a small cistern and a courtyard with columns, the **palaestra,** probably a games area for athletes, just north of which was a complex of baths.

On leaving Curium, take the road west towards Paphos. Past vineyards, on winding cliffside roads, you come to **Petra tou Romiou** (29 miles from Limassol), better known as the legendary Birthplace of Aphrodite. A couple of large rocks mark the place where the love goddess swirled out of the sea. This scenic spot is appropriately romantic, especially towards sunset. A tourist pavilion stocked with refreshments is discreetly hidden just uphill. **61**

Modern-day Aphrodite? Legend has it the Goddess of Love sprang from the waves at Petra tou Romiou.

Troodos Mountains

The Troodos (pronounced TROW-dohss) chain in west-central Cyprus is the island's principal upland area—providing most of its fresh water, plus welcome cool air and scenery in summer and skiing in winter. From foothills with rushing streams and orchards to perched villages surrounded by vast tracts of forest, the Troodos mountains offer a wealth of natural beauty. The area is renowned for its dozens of monasteries (steep retreats from marauders of the past) and the resort hotels and spas that add to nature's attractions.

Pano Platres, or "Platres" as it's called, makes an ideal base for visiting the whole Troodos region. About 1½ hours by car from Nicosia or 45 minutes from Limassol, the little town with its hotels, restaurants and boutiques occupies a charming and shady mountain site. The population varies from 500 to upwards of 1,500 in the high summer season, when the people of Limassol come here to escape from seaside heat and humidity. The Platres Festival, featuring handicrafts and folk events, attracts local people and holiday-makers alike.

But there's nothing brash or vulgar about this quiet resort centre; a century ago, it was a favourite rest spot of fatigued British troops. Walking is the most popular sport—though the occasional snake may cross your path. A fairly relaxed and scenic possibility is the half-mile hike up to **Caledonian Falls,** a pretty if not spectacular cascade. Other points of interest around Platres include **Phini,** a charming village about 3½ miles away, with sinuous

Troodos mountainsides are often terraced for fruit-growing.

streets, friendly people and an informal folklore museum, open when the owner is home.

You might follow a hand-lettered sign about fifty steps uphill to the premises of a "lady potter", a local woman who makes traditional, Cypriot-style red-clay ceramics. The whole family is employed in this flourishing cottage industry, and they are more than happy to show visitors their simple dirt-floored workroom and wares.

Also close by is **Troodhitissa Monastery,** reached after a 5-mile drive through towering evergreen forests on a road that is well paved but much too narrow for the two-way traffic it supports. The original church of the monastery was built in 1250 by two monks living as hermits in a nearby cave, who apparently were inspired by a miraculous vision of the Virgin Mary. The church was twice destroyed by fire; the present edifice dates from 1731, and the surrounding buildings with rooms for guests are modern.

The triple-aisled church is attractive although unremarkable; its chief icon is a silver-covered image of the Virgin, which receives its share of kisses from Cypriot visitors, as do all important icons on the island. Next to it is the holy belt *(ayia zoni),* a leather belt decorated with silver which reputedly has the power to make women fertile. Crowds throng to Troodhitissa on August 15 (Assumption Day), feast day of the Virgin Mary.

The minute summer-winter settlement of **Troodos** nestles just under Cyprus's highest peak, Mount Olympus (6,401 ft.). At an altitude of 5,500 feet, Troodos is the highest resort on the island and its skiing mecca. On the way from Platres (5 miles to the south), you'll pass Government Lodge, a rather austere stone Scottish-style hunting lodge used by the president as a summer residence. The building was erected in the late 19th century and for a couple of years during the construction the French poet Arthur Rimbaud worked here as a foreman—a fact commemorated by a plaque mounted in the 1940s. Troodos has a few tennis courts—there's a tournament in summer—and some modest hotels. But most of the activity is on the "main street", where weekend day-trippers crowd a tiny area to browse in the stalls and small shops and eat and drink in one of the cafés with terraces that serve fish and chips and *souvlaki.* It's usually fun to stop for lunch here, but swarms of flies in early autumn can detract from the appeal of the place.

As in Platres, walking is the main entertainment, although there are a few drowsy-looking horses and ponies to hire for half an hour or more. The pine-scented air is dry and agreeable, but the scenery is eerie: huge, twisted varieties of Aleppo pine struggle up out of the reddish clay and rocky cliffs, creating an almost otherworldly effect after the gracious glades of Platres. You may want to drive up to Mt. Olympus for a vast view. On a clear day you can see all Cyprus through a telescope at the top.

From Troodos you can go north to the delightful little town of Kakopetria or northwest towards Kykko Monastery. **Kakopetria** nestles in a valley of the Troodos foothills.

With about 1,300 inhabitants in the off-season, more in summer, it's a favourite weekend retreat for residents of Nicosia —cooler and more charming than the rather bleak and arid countryside around the capital. Old, balconied houses, an ancient flour mill and shady squares make this a colourful halting place.

The most interesting sight in the area is **St. Nicholas of the Roof** *(Ayios Nikolaos tis Steyis)*, a monastery with a remarkable gabled and shingled roof, obviously repaired many times over the centuries. The church and monastery (uninhabited at present) occupy an attractively flowered garden site above a green gorge with a stream rushing below. The gardener keeps the keys of the church and will let visitors inside. The frescoes here are exceptionally lively compositions of various periods from the 11th to 17th centuries. Note the facial expressions, especially in panels relating to the life of Christ—such as the *Nativity* and the *Entry into Jerusalem*. They show a good deal of drama and much more human concern than earlier Byzantine conventions allowed.

There's plenty to see on the way to Kykko, including splendid views—if you have the skill and stamina to negotiate all the narrow roads with hairpin turns. The first small town after Troodos is **Prodhromos**, set 4,600 feet above sea level among pines, fruit orchards and vineyards. Well-known for its Forestry College, Prodhromos has a few adequate hotels and restaurants frequented by hardy hikers. You may want to visit the experimental orchard at TRIKOU-CHIA, where new varieties of fruit are cultivated.

A few miles and many hairpin turns further north towards Kykko, you come to **Pedhoulas,** another appealing perched village with several hotels and cafés. Pedhoulas is famed for its cherry orchards, and in spring Cypriots come from all over the island to witness the spectacle of tens of thousands of trees in blossom. The 15th-century **Archangel Michael Church** occupies an impressive site on a steep hill overlooking the valley. The most remarkable of the frescoes here is one of an out-sized Angel Michael, brandishing his sword. Near the hotels and village centre stands an ancient cedar tree of vast proportions. The Forestry Department recently calculated its age at well over 450.

It's 12 miles from Pedhoulas to **Kykko Monastery** (road

Kykko monastery shimmers in gold.

conditions slightly better than Prodhromos–Pedhoulas). Far from the world on its mountaintop, with pine forests all around, this is the best-known of all the island's monasteries and a pilgrimage place for Cypriots and tourists alike. Like so many others on Cyprus, the monastery was founded by a hermit in A.D. 1100. The reigning emperor, Alexis Comnenos, presented Kykko with a land grant and a precious icon of the Virgin Mary, said to have been painted by St. Luke himself. Several fires during the centuries destroyed the monastery, but the icon managed to survive them all and is now covered over with gilded silver. The belief that the image has magical rain-making powers persists, and in times of drought nearby farmers and their families occasionally join the monks to pray, in a plea for rain.

Kykko was famed in the Orthodox world and revered by Tsarist Russia (a Russian noblewoman donated the bells in the belfry in 1860). The monastery reportedly served as the main communications and supply base for the 1950s freedom movement rebels (EOKA) under Georgios Grivas—which is not surprising given the rather remote situation and difficult access. The buildings you see today are very white, bright, even modern looking, with many new rooms for pilgrims and guests—though there are fewer monks at Kykko now than in the days when Archbishop Makarios was a novice.

The church presents a lively scene, especially at weekends, with mass baptisms, bearded priests in profusion, screaming babies and—of course—a crowd lined up in front of the sanctuary to venerate the holy icons. On the right after entering, you'll see the original icon of the Virgin given by Alexis Comnenos, and next to it a protruding arm of blackened bronze, supposedly that of a thoughtless infidel who tried to light a cigarette from one of the icon's lamps and was punished by seeing his arm wither and turn to metal. Offerings to the Virgin—ranging from expensive jewellery to simple beeswax ex votos—hang here in profusion.

Outside dozens of little knick-knack stands line the way to a pleasant café terrace.

A road leads a mile uphill to the **Tomb of Archbishop Makarios III.** The political-activist ethnarch lies buried in a cave. He chose the place long before his death. The site offers sweeping views of deserted hills and valleys—an isolated spot except for the streams of tourists in buses and cars. The modern chapel nearby was designed by Andreas and Iakovos Philippou.

Home of the moufflon, a mountain sheep, and the cedar tree, **Cedar Valley** is an attraction for nature-lovers about 9 miles west of Kykko. While Lebanon is traditionally associated with the cedar, the tree is native to Cyprus, too. The Cedar Valley reserve alone boasts 50,000 towering trees *(Cedrus brevifolia)*, some centuries old. Together with the Aleppo pine, plane and gold oak, they provide miles of sylvan hiking areas (those with less time or energy can simply drive through). The most venerable cedar here is around 850 years old, according to the Cyprus Forestry Department; this methuselah of nature reaches 100 feet into the air. **67**

Paphos

This bright, cheerful seaside town is fast becoming Cyprus's most attractive holiday spot —its small port and resort offering both scenery and fascinating antique sites. In fact, Paphos is a city of many layers, with traces of the past constantly being unearthed. Fortunately, the hustle-bustle of tourism has not yet overrun Paphos. The population still hovers around 11,000 or so— and, while building is booming, it's not on a high-rise scale.

Legend attributes the founding of Palea Paphos to the priest-king Cinyras. A temple was built to Aphrodite here in Mycenaean times, and the city-kingdom gained renown as the centre of Aphrodite's cult. Earthquakes destroyed the temple sometime in the late 12th century B.C., but it was rebuilt soon after by King Agapenor from Arcadia in the Peloponnese, who was shipwrecked in the area on his return from the Trojan War. Agapenor subsequently set himself up as king of Paphos.

Under the Romans, Cyprus was governed from Nea Paphos; it was here that the Proconsul Sergius Paulus was converted to Christianity (see p. 17). The last king of Old Paphos, Ni-

cocles, established the new port town of Nea Paphos late in the 4th century B.C., though Palea Paphos remained the centre of Aphrodite worship until the 4th century A.D. Within a hundred years of its founding, Nea Paphos surpassed Salamis as chief city of Cyprus, continuing in importance through Roman times. Earthquakes in 332 and 342 and Saracen attacks in the 7th century forced most of the population inland to Ktima, though Nea Paphos was not completely abandoned until 1372, following the Genoese invasion.

A small seaport for crusaders and others, Paphos languished as a miserable place with a poor reputation. However, the population gradually increased to over 2,000 by the late 19th century. And the harbour was dredged in 1908, attracting further maritime commerce. Paphos continued to grow and prosper, and in spite of some damage in the 1974 war, it bounced back to attract not only tourists but new Cypriot settlers as well.

On a beautiful hilltop site 140 feet above sea level, **Ktima** is a clean, lively and modern area of Paphos, graced with Neoclassical-style school and bank buildings, green open spaces and a big market. On the road

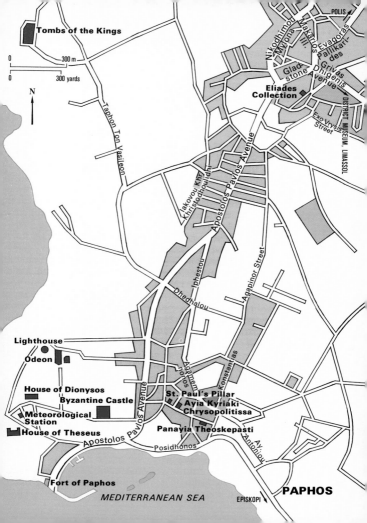

Tombs of the Kings

POLIS

0 ——— 300 m

0 ——— 300 yards

N

Taphon Ton Vasileon

Nikodimou Mylona Makarios III. Evagoras Pallikari-des

Gladstone

Grivas Dhigenis Avenue

Eliades Collection

Exo Vrysis Street

DISTRICT MUSEUM, LIMASSOL

Iakovou Kritsiodhou lidh

Apostolos Pavlos Avenue

Ifhestou

Agapinor Street

Dhedhalou

Lighthouse

Odeon

Agamemnonos

Konstantias

House of Dionysos

Byzantine Castle

St. Paul's Pillar

Ayia Kyriaki Chrysopolitissa

Meteorological Station

House of Theseus

Panayia Theoskepasti

Apostolos Pavlos Avenue

Posidhonos

Ayi Antoniou

Fort of Paphos

PAPHOS

MEDITERRANEAN SEA

EPISKOPI

to Limassol is the small **Paphos District Museum** (Dhigenis Avenue), displaying ever-expanding archaeological collections that continue to grow as excavations in the Paphos area progress. Among the outstanding exhibits are the sarcophagus and bones of a 20-year-old female from nearby Emba, who was about five feet five —an exceptional height for a woman in the 3rd millennium B.C.; and a striking Hellenistic lion that looks more pussycat than wild cat. Take note of the votive figurines, terracotta male and female heads of uncommon beauty (Cypro-archaic and classical periods) and the jewellery, pottery, glass and coins from various periods. Many objects come from famed local sites such as the House of Dionysos and Tombs of the Kings. The beautiful marble Greco-Roman Aphrodite was dredged from the sea near Nea Paphos. Roman, too, is the headless yet impressive marble statue of an armed Aphrodite.

The **George S. Eliades Collection** in Exo Vrysis Street near the Bishop's Palace represents a touching labour of love. Professor Eliades and his wife welcome visitors at "reasonable" hours daily (you can ring up from the nearby tourist office) to their 1894 house, where they display a large collection of local palaeontological, archaeological and folklore objects. The fossils date back millions of years, while the bridal chamber contains charming furniture and locally made costumes of more recent vintage (18th and 19th centuries). You'll see a huge wine cask, an olive press and ovens for cooking bread or meat out in the rear—and, in the grounds, several rock tombs from the 3rd century B.C. Mr. Eliades finishes up his enthusiastic explanations by showing off a large coin collection begun in 1957. (It's polite to buy a booklet or give money, since the Eliadeses are totally dependent on personal resources and not helped by outside funds.)

Nea Paphos offers plenty of excitement for archaeology buffs. Off the main Apostolos Pavlos Avenue (descending to the harbour), you'll find **St. Paul's Pillar.** Here, according to local legend, St. Paul was tied and lashed 39 times for preaching the Gospel. Just afterwards the apostle managed to meet the Roman governor, Sergius Paulus, and convert

Paphos' Old Fort commands a fine view of the waterfront.

him to Christianity by blinding the sorcerer Elymas.

To the east, the early 16th-century church of **Ayia Kyriaki Chrysopolitissa** (Blessed Virgin Mary of the Golden City) stands on the site of an early Christian basilica whose foundations are still being uncovered; the vast main structure was 164 feet long and 131 feet wide—making the basilica one of the largest in Cyprus. From behind a wire enclosure outside the present church, visitors can view traces of mosaics from the 4th century A.D.—largely inscriptions and geometric designs. Vestiges of the Gothic church that replaced it are visible nearby.

Just a few steps east, Panayia Theoskepasti (Holy Virgin Veiled by God) serves as the parish church of Kato Paphos. Built high on a rock in 1923, this modern church stands on the site of a much older sanctuary. Little is remarkable about it save the legend that explains its name: each time the dreaded Saracens raided during the 7th to 10th centuries, they left the original Panayia Theoskepasti untouched, since a cloud miraculously appeared to obscure it from view.

West of Apostolos Pavlos Avenue lies the **Byzantine Castle**, otherwise known as Forty Columns *(Saranda Kolones);* until excavation in 1957 proved this was a fortress, it looked like little more than forty columns around a mound of earth, hence the name. Buried here were a large keep with four columns, a moat and thick exterior walls—all built in the 7th century A.D. and destroyed by an earthquake in 1222. Supposedly it was the place where Richard the Lionheart defeated Isaac Comnenos in 1191.

A short distance west, the **House of Dionysos** has spectacular mosaic decorations. This 3rd-century A.D. Roman villa was unearthed in 1962, and although the 20-odd rooms around a peristyle atrium had no walls left, many mosaic floors remain, a legacy of the rich man with good taste who commissioned them. Greatly damaged during the 1974 invasion, the pavements were reconstituted and a protective metal roof was erected.

You'll see marvellously preserved **mosaics** of mythological subjects. The Roman owner must have loved wine, the big theme, which explains the name House of Dionysos—after the god of wine. As depicted, the legend shows Dionysos introducing wine to the legendary king of Athens,

Ikarios, in the company of a nymph, Akmi. Ikarios unwisely treated the locals to some of this new potion, and they became the first human drunkards. These novice bibbers became totally smashed (they thought they were poisoned) and finally killed Ikarios. Other lively mosaics show Apollo and Daphne, Pyramus and Thisbe, the figure of Zeus as an eagle making off with the youth Ganymede, and much more.

Especially appealing are the hunting scenes in the atrium (bear, panther, moufflon, deer, boar, wild sheep) and the vineyard, flower and landscape scenes—all of which attest to the healthy, robust enjoyment of nature and the senses by both the house's owner and the artist. While digging for the shelter foundations was under way, a black and white Hellenistic pebble mosaic was found under the Roman mosaics. Reset in an adjoining room, it shows a sea monster with dolphins.

North of the House of Dionysos, on the slope of Fabrica Hill, you'll see the **Odeon**, a reconstruction of the original 2nd-century A.D. Roman theatre, destroyed by earthquake. With a lighthouse behind it, this picturesque semicircular structure faces east; 11 of the

New or Old?

The several names and places associated with Paphos—continuously inhabited since 1,500 B.C.—are enough to make the mind reel. First came Palea Paphos (Old Paphos), situated about 10 miles east of the modern town at Kouklia. There are few visible remains of this settlement, which flourished from the 15th to 4th centuries B.C. Nea Paphos (New Paphos) then took over as political centre, reaching its zenith in Roman times. Preserved here are ruins of theatres, an agora, several villas and early Christian churches. Nea Paphos extends inland for about two miles from today's port area, called Kato Paphos (Lower Paphos). By the time Nea Paphos was finally abandoned in 1372, the real "new" Paphos, known as Ktima, had grown up just over a mile away. But then, there's so much development and construction around Nea Paphos and Kato Paphos nowadays that you'll have to forget trying to think of old or new!

original 25 tiers of seats have been rebuilt, and 1,250 spectators can be accommodated for outdoor performances.

Adjacent to the Odeon are ruins of the **Asklepeion**, a 73

temple and clinic dedicated to the god of healing, Asklepios. This precursor of the health farm apparently prescribed a spartan regimen of tepid water, followed by several days of vegetarian food; cured patients were supposed to offer a cock in thanks. A handsome statue of the god of healing found here is now in the Paphos District Museum.

Just south-west of the House of Dionysos, past the meteorological station, the **House of Theseus** (excavated since 1965 by the Polish Archaeological Mission) also boasts some important mosaics, such as the circular, stylized picture of Theseus killing the Minotaur.

Earthquakes, squatters and vandals destroyed the grand villa, believed to have been the residence of the Roman proconsuls (governors) from the 2nd to 6th centuries A.D. It was obviously palatial, with long paved rooms, marble statues and baths. Most of the objects found here are now exhibited in the Paphos District Museum. The large building complex under excavation may have replaced an earlier edifice, where, it is said, Sergius Paulus was converted to Christianity in A.D. 45 by the apostles Paul and Barnabas.

Further down at the port of Kato Paphos, you'll pass the customs house, some cheery seaside restaurants and tavernas. You can't miss the sturdy **Fort of Paphos,** rebuilt by the Turks in 1592 on the site of an earlier medieval castle. A quick visit suffices, since empty cells, dungeons and good views from the top are the only points of interest here. Heading east along the waterfront, you reach a pleasant resort area where hotel pools and beach facilities are accessible for a small fee; a couple of miles further, over a very rough road, is the Yeroskipos Beach tourist facility, with an attractive grassy area and taverna.

Situated to the north-west of Nea Paphos at Paleokastra is the necropolis of the old Roman town, known today as the **Tombs of the Kings.** Scores of burial chambers lie below ground level, carved from the ruddy rock that slopes down to the sea. Although the tombs were not royal (Paphos had no kings at the time of their construction, from the 3rd century B.C. to the 3rd century A.D.), they are certainly impressive enough. A large map posted at the entry indicates the position of the most interesting burial chambers, which are grouped not too far from one another. There's an air of gran-

Elaborate courtyards grace Paphos' Tombs of the Kings.

deur about these rock-hewn tombs that make our modern-day mausoleums look merely pretentious. Those marked with a cross served as the last resting place of early Christians.

The most elaborate chambers have courtyards with peristyles of Doric columns and decorative entablatures carved from the living rock in imitation of the dwellings of Nea Paphos. **75**

Environs of Paphos

Two miles east of town, on the road from Nea Paphos to the Temple of Aphrodite at Palea Paphos, you come to **Yeroskipos** ("Sacred Garden"). Once a garden dedicated to Aphrodite, it served as a halting place for devotees of the goddess en route from the port of Nea Paphos to the temple at Palea Paphos. Yeroskipos later became a silk-manufacturing centre, due to the many mulberry trees here (operations ceased after World War II). Now the tiny town is famed for its Turkish Delight, the ultra-sweet *loukoumi*.

In the central square stands the church of **Ayia Paraskevi**, a small basilica with five domes (an unusual number), built in the 11th century in honour of the martyr-saint, Paraskevi. A shoemaker beside the church is the affable keeper of the key and tour guide. He'll point out 15th-century murals (notice the *Raising of Lazarus* and *Christ Entering Jerusalem*); scenes of the Passion, including the *Last Supper* and *Christ in the Garden of Gethsemane;* as well as a 13th-century *Dormition of the Virgin.* The church's most important icon (15th century) has two holy images: A *Virgin and Child* with a *Crucifixion* on the reverse side.

In an old restored house nearby is the **Museum of Folk Art.** Typical of an 18th-century rich Cypriot's villa, it has an upper storey surrounded with handsome wooden balconies. The house once belonged to Andreas Zimboulakis, British consular agent for Paphos—a post Andreas and then his son held from 1799 to 1865. Museum displays include gourds that kept children afloat while they learned to swim, even jars of carob honey, from which you can take a taste. You'll see agricultural tools, elaborately carved furniture, a lovely 18th-century painted grandfather clock, and other items.

From Yeroskipos, take the Limassol road 8 miles and turn off at KOUKLIA, once Palea Paphos, where the cult of Aphrodite took place. The love-goddess rites flourished at the **Sanctuary of Aphrodite** from very early times. Homer described the yearly spring festival—the Mysteries—which contributed much to the fame and coffers of Cyprus, as pilgrims came from all over the ancient world. Now in the Cyprus Museum in Nicosia, a conical stone symbolizing the goddess (her beauty was too great to represent literally) was the symbolic centre of Aphrodite worship.

The Love Goddess

She may have been born at Cythera and wafted by wind and waves to Paphos. Or she may have sprung from the foam at Petra tou Romiou to the east. Whatever the case, the ancients considered Palea Paphos to be the true home of the goddess of love and beauty. In the *Odyssey* Homer wrote, "But laughter-loving Aphrodite went to Cyprus and to Paphos, where is her precinct and fragrant altars". She was considered a great beauty and was depicted as such through the centuries. The Renaissance painter Botticelli saw her as a delicate Venus (Roman name) poised on a seashell, riding the waves. A Homeric hymn describes the scene:

> *The breath of the west wind bore her*
> *Over the sounding sea,*
> *Up from the delicate foam,*
> *To wave-ringed Cyprus, her isle.*

In most legends, Aphrodite was the wife of Hephaestus, god of the forge (Vulcan to the Romans). As mother of Aeneas, she helped her son to safety during the siege of Troy. Eros (Cupid) was also her child—a capricious, naughty little soul who caused havoc between lovers.

As for her own lovers, they included Ares (Mars), the rather unsympathetic god of war, and Adonis, symbol of beauty and love. As the myth relates, she fell for Adonis from his very birth, but Persephone, goddess of the underworld, would not part with him; the dispute was taken to Zeus, who decided this gorgeous youth would spend half a year with each goddess. Finally, Aphrodite saw Adonis wounded by a boar (hunting was his favourite sport) and he expired to sink into the underworld in a pool of blood.

Alas, little remains of romance in the ruins on view in Kouklia, a small farming community. Aphrodite seems to have wafted away on a zephyr, the way she came. Archaeologists have been at work here since the late 19th century, uncovering the sanctuary—believed to lie largely under some surrounding farm dwellings. You can distinguish north and south stoas or halls, and some cyclopean blocks which formed a Bronze Age wall.

The Château de Covocle nearby—originally a Lusignan fort, and then a Turkish manor house and farm—houses the collection of the **Palea Paphos Museum.** Although many of the valuable finds from the sanctuary have been taken to Nicosia (such as a mosaic of *Leda and the Swan,* once stolen from here and later recovered), there are still some ceramics and other objects of minor interest.

Excursions
Just 7 miles north-west of Paphos, the scenic cliff-top holiday village of CORAL BAY provides relaxation by the sea (with tavernas and pink-tinged sandy beach). Inland to the north, you might head for a real treat on Cyprus—Polis and the Baths of Aphrodite.

A jog off the Polis road takes you to the **Monastery of Ayios Neophytos,** 6 miles north of Paphos. On a peaceful, wooded hillside, the large monastery has several residential buildings and a domed basilica with some good 15th- and 16th-century frescoes and icons and an intricately carved iconostasis (partition separating choir from nave). In 1750, the bones of the hermit-monk St. Neophytos were removed from his tomb to repose here.

The monastery grew up around the **Englistra** (Hermitage)—a cave dwelling in the hillside opposite the church where St. Neophytos (1134–1214) lived in seclusion. Author of religious and historical works, Neophytos went into retreat here in the late 12th century, carving the troglodytic dwelling with his own hands and supervising the decoration of chapel, sanctuary and cell with superb fresco paintings. One scene shows Neophytos himself, flanked by the archangels Michael and Gabriel. The frescoes are badly lit. To see them, bring a torch (flashlight) or ask for assistance.

About 20 miles further on by the main road north, you'll come to POLIS, an unassuming little township that looks back on a more glorious past.

Monastery of Ayios Neophytos near Paphos welcomes visitors and pilgrims.

Known as Marion in ancient times, it was a city-kingdom of Cyprus that boasted rich gold and copper mines. Next stop going west on the Akamas peninsula could be LACHI, if you'd like to try windsurfing from the water-sports centre here.

If a vote were taken for the scenic high point of a visit to Cyprus, the winner might well be the **Baths of Aphrodite** *(Loutra tis Aphroditis)*, a place of stunning natural beauty. The ever-narrower signposted road takes you right to the tourist pavilion. From here it's a short walk up through peaceful woods to the pool within a small glade associated with the goddess of love. Various springs feed this cool and romantic spot—a bower of greenery where Aphrodite had legendary trysts with many young men; rejected suitors supposedly walked a few paces to a spring on the east side to bathe in cold water.

You can continue 2 miles by foot or boat (the only ways to go) to the Fontana Amorosa, or Fountain of Love. But if Aphrodite ever played her love scenes here, you wouldn't know it today; the "fontana" is only one of a group of muddy wells, used by goatherds to water their charges. An easier and more scenic

occupation would be to have drinks or lunch back at the Tourist Pavilion, where you can enjoy a sweeping view of turquoise-to-ultramarine waters from on high. The swimming and snorkelling off the shore below is superb.

While the monastery of Panayia Chrysorroyiatissa may be reached via some rather perilous mountain roads from Troodos, it's much easier to make the excursion from Paphos. Again take the road north to Polis, turning off to POLEMI and continuing on through PANO PANAYIA, the birthplace in 1913 of Mihail Mouskos, who became the famed archbishop and later president, Makarios III.

Panayia Chrysorroyiatissa ("Our Lady of the Golden Pomegranate") perches on a hilly site with green forest around it. The monk Ignatios founded the monastery in 1152; the present complex dates from the late 18th century, restored in 1955. The cloister is built on an unusual triangular plan (most are quadrangles). Within the enclosure stands the church, noted for its elaborately carved iconostasis. A heavy silver-gilt case encloses the chief icon of the Virgin, framed in silver, a favourite of criminals and outlaws seeking divine help.

Northern Cyprus

The Turkish-occupied Cyprus, comprising around 37 per cent of the island, boasts some lovely scenery and magnificent antiquities. It has a more "Byzantine" character: a somewhat indolent and sensuous approach to life prevails, in contrast to the pragmatic and energetic lifestyle of the Greek south.

From Nicosia, you can see the lovely blue-green rise of the Kyrenia chain; the peak called Pentadaktylos (Five-Fingered Mountain) is outstanding not for its height (around 2,400 ft.) but for its silhouette. As Cypriot legend would have it, "Five-Fingered Mountain" bears the handprint of the hero Dhigenis. In *Bitter Lemons,* Lawrence Durrell calls the chain *"par excellence* the Gothic range, for it is studded with crusader castles pitched on the dizzy spines of the mountains, commanding the roads which run over the saddles between".

The most spectacular of these Gothic high points is undoubtedly **St. Hilarion Castle,** clinging to its 2,200-foot peak like a splendid conglomeration of towers and crenellated walls from a child's fairy-tale book. The castle evolved from a church and monastery built in the 10th century to honour the hermit-saint Hilarion, who fled to the locality when Arabs advanced on Syria. Byzantines put up the original structures and Lusignans fortified and extended them. St. Hilarion occupies a superb vantage point —which means you have to do a lot of walking (mostly uphill) to reach the castle, which is situated on three distinct levels.

On the lower level are garrison, stables and cisterns; the middle level is the site of the small restored 10th-century Byzantine church, and traces of a loggia, kitchens and living quarters; the upper level (after a dauntingly steep climb) offers Frankish-Byzantine ruins.

Next in the chain of Frankish castles in the Kyrenia range is **Buffavento,** the highest at 3,100 feet. Dismantled by the Venetians, Buffavento is a heap of crumbling stone, whipped by the wind. It's accessible by road but can also be reached by donkey or foot (the climb up takes just under an hour).

Kantara Castle, about 40 miles to the east, completes this trio of fortifications; it's a ruin, too, but better preserved than Buffavento. A narrow road goes up to the top.

With a horseshoe-shaped harbour and a handsome castle

lookout, the old port town of **Kyrenia** retains some of its original charm. The massive Byzantine **castle** looms large at water's edge; it was rebuilt by the Lusignans around 1208 and later fortified by Venetians.

The castle walls enclose a Byzantine chapel and the tomb of the Turkish admiral Sadik Pasha, who wrested the castle from the Venetians in 1570. Here, too, are royal apartments, prison cells and dungeons. Be sure to have a look at the **Kyrenia Ship,** one of the oldest vessels ever recovered from the sea. This Greek trading ship sank off the coast of Cyprus in 300 B.C. Discovered in 1965 by Andreas Kariolou, a sponge diver and amateur underwater archaeologist, it was salvaged four years later by the University of Pennsylvania Museum Expedition for the National Geographic Society. The hull, reconstructed over a period of six years, has been placed on exhibition together with some of the objects carried on board —wine jars, mill stones, cooking utensils—even some ancient almonds.

Bellapais Abbey (3 miles east of Kyrenia) has long been known as one of the most beautiful spots in Cyprus. Raised on a cliff over 700 feet above the dark-blue sea,

the 13th-century abbey (now largely in ruins) enjoys sweeping views and an idyllic setting of cypress trees, palms, orange, lemon and olive trees. The Lusignans founded the "Abbey of Peace" *(Abbaye de la Paix),* and their coat-of-arms appears on the monastic buildings in French Gothic style, for they protected the Augustinian Order established here. The church with its nave and two aisles was constructed for Latin worship. Although the cloister has no vaulting, its arches are intact: note the perfection of the carved decoration—especially the animal and human figures. In a good state of preservation, the vaulted refectory is a vast room of 36 by 98 feet. The beautiful Gothic interior preserves a rose window and vestiges of the wooden benches where the monks sat at table.

Surrounding the abbey is BELLAPAIS village, where Lawrence Durrell lived for two years or more, drawing inspiration for *Bitter Lemons.*

On the eastern coast of Cyprus, **Famagusta** was only a village when Christian refugees from Acre arrived in 1291. A century later it was famed as a city of riches, peopled with merchants, courtesans and others who lived fast and loose. Venetians and Cypriots defend- **83**

Handsome Roman statues adorn ruins at Salamis.

ed the city against invading Turks in the bloody siege of Famagusta (1570–71), which ended in betrayal. The Venetian governor, Marcantonio Bragadino, surrendered the starving city only to be flayed alive. The Turks stuffed his skin and promenaded this gruesome relic around town. They then went on to massacre thousands of people.

Long the most important port in Cyprus and a major tourist centre before the Turkish invasion in 1974, today Famagusta is but a shadow of its former self, all Greek Cypriots had to leave the city for the south. The old town and Venetian fortifications remain Famagusta's most interesting sights. Down by the harbour stands the famous **Citadel,** or Tower of Othello, associated with one Christoforo Moro, a 16th-century Lieutenant-Governor of Cyprus and the possible model for Shakespeare's troubled Moor. Surrounded by a moat, the tower sports four round corner turrets, a 92-foot-long grand hall and a barrel-arched entry adorned with the winged lion of St. Mark—a fitting setting for the Othello story.

To the north-west, **Martinengo Bastion** proved so impenetrable that even the Turks were intimidated in 1570 and never mounted an attack.

While the Venetians gave Famagusta its fortifications, it was the Lusignans who built the city's churches, which at one time numbered 365. In the centre of the old town stands the **former cathedral,** which has been converted into the Lala Mustafa Pasha Mosque. Under construction from 1298 to 1326, this fine example of French Gothic style sports a minaret, though it has suffered few other changes. Here the Lusignan rulers of Cyprus were crowned kings of Jerusalem. The western façade with its superb Gothic doorways and towers has been compared to French architectural masterpieces of the period.

A few arches nearby mark the site of the **Venetian Governor's Palace** *(Palazzo del Provveditore),* taken over from the Lusignans and expanded. In the courtyard here the brave Bragadino met his death.

Salamis (5½ miles north of Famagusta) ranks with the most magnificent of Cyprus's antique sites. For some 2,000 years Salamis enjoyed preeminence among the city-kingdoms of Cyprus, at one time counting 100,000 citizens. Under the name Constantia, it became capital of Cyprus in A.D. 395. Constantia lost population after several earthquakes inflicted serious damage and the city, raided by Arabs, was abandoned altogether in 647.

The ancient centre of Salamis extends east of the Famagusta road to the seafront, while the necropolis is to the west. The visible ruins date from Hellenistic, Roman and Byzantine times and cover a wide area.

Not far from the entrance is the site of Ayios Epiphanios, a basilica of the 4th century A.D. Little survives, save for the foundations and the tomb where Epiphanios, Bishop of Constantia, was laid to rest.

Farther along, the Roman **Theatre** (2nd century A.D.) probably succeeded an earlier Greek structure. Now partially restored, it is the largest ancient theatre to be discovered to date in Cyprus, and could once hold as many as 15,000 spectators.

The **Gymnasium** and adjacent **Palaestra,** with the Public Baths, are among the best remnants of antiquity to be seen in the island. The graceful marble columns in Corinthian style have been re-erected, and a Byzantine marble pavement revealed. In the **baths** area, you can distinguish cold rooms, hot-air rooms and the *caldarium,* where water was heated by furnaces beneath the floor. The water itself was channelled from Kythrea, 37 miles away, via the Roman aqueduct still standing.

Known as the **Tombs of the Kings,** the necropolis of Salamis contains royal burial chambers uncovered in the 1960s with all they contained —ceramics, precious objects, the chariots that carried the bodies of the dead and the skeletons of the horses that pulled them. (The animals were sacrificed.)

What to Do

Sports and sightseeing excursions fill most visitors' time, with a few shopping forays for good measure, or even a short cruise along the coast. Cyprus also has a unique folklore and cuisine to discover. Attend a rousing village festival, see a display of Cypriot dancing or sample *mezedes* in a waterfront restaurant—the choice is yours on Aphrodite's island.

Sports

A beneficent climate, varied landscape and marvellous beaches make Cyprus ideal for sports of all kinds—including even skiing, on a very limited scale. Only golfers need desist —since irrigation poses problems. But the outstanding water sports possibilities make up for any shortcomings.

Water Sports

For specific details about facilities available at particular resorts, consult the Cyprus Tourism Organization.

Swimming. The water is limpid and tempting, and beach-scapes vary from vast smooth sandy stretches to stimulating swimming off the rocks, with sand and rocks sometimes in the same place. Excellent public sand beaches sponsored by the Cyprus Tourism Organization are beautifully laid out with grass around them. Amenities include changing rooms, bar-restaurants, basket- and volley-ball courts and, often, sports equipment for hire. You'll find tourist beaches at Ayia Napa, east of Larnaca at Dhekelia, east of Limassol at Dassoudi, and east of Paphos at Yeros-kipos Beach.

Other beautiful sites include Petra tou Romiou (informal bathing under Aphrodite's Rock, with a restaurant uphill); the Baths of Aphrodite, west of Polis (spectacular setting, tourist pavilion restaurant); and Coral Bay, north of Paphos (lovely scenery, sand and rocks, restaurant).

All of the better hotels have excellent freshwater pools, some Olympic size. Several allow non-residents to use the facilities for a reasonable fee or for patronage of the poolside snack bar.

Snorkelling and Scuba-diving. The unpolluted waters around Cyprus are perfect for snorkelling and underwater

Limpid blue waters lap at the inviting beach of Ayia Napa.

photography, and there's an abundance of small fish to be seen around the rocks. Diving centres with facilities and instruction exist at Paphos, Coral Beach, Lachi (near Polis), Fig Tree Bay, Larnaca and Ayia Napa. Several hotels near Limassol and Larnaca also offer diving possibilities.

Windsurfing and Water-skiing. You can practice these sports at public and hotel beaches during the warm season; rental of equipment and cost of instruction may vary from resort to resort. A thrilling variant of water-skiing, parasailing is offered around Larnaca and Limassol.

Boating and Sailing. You can hire a motor boat of your own or join an organized group for a day's motor-launch cruise offshore. Inquire at the marinas of Larnaca, Limassol, Ayia Napa and Paphos. There are sailing clubs at Larnaca, Limassol and Paphos, and many hotels and resort centres have sailboats and pedaloes for hire.

Fishing. Amateur anglers need no licence for sport fishing at sea (including spear fishing), and boats with or without captains and equipment can be hired in many localities. Local fishermen go for red mullet, white bream, grouper, pickerel and amberjack. While billfish

and swordfish may be caught in Cyprus waters, you'll need to hire a special boat and guide.

Cyprus has no native freshwater fish, but several dammed-up areas have been stocked with trout, carp and other fish.

Other Sports

Tennis. Better hotels invariably provide tennis courts (clay or asphalt) for guests, often available to non-residents for a small fee. There are several courts at Nicosia's Field Club and at the Lapatsa Sporting Centre in Tseri (15 minutes from Nicosia).

Horse Riding. With an indoor arena and outdoor paddock, the Lapatsa Sporting Centre offers a full equitation programme, from dressage and show jumping to cross-country riding (courses for beginners to advanced, adults and children). In a totally different category, children or others can ride a horse or pony to sightsee around Troodos (nags are for hire by the half-hour—usually on weekends).

Walking and Hiking. You can trek through the Troodos chain and foothills, past pleasant mountain streams, many delightful villages and viewpoints. The Cyprus Tourism Organization distributes maps and information on itineraries.

Tours organized from abroad propose excursions in the area, from a base in Pano Platres or Troodos.

Winter Sports

Promoters of the Troodos mountains resort area would like to see more people take advantage of winter as a time to visit Cyprus, when lower prices are in force. Lifts provide access to several runs on Mt. Olympus, and more are being developed all the time. Cross-country skiing is also possible. Depending on snow conditions, the ski season runs from January to early March.

Spectator Sports

Car Racing. A big and exciting event in European racing, the 72-hour international Cyprus Rally in September attracts up to 80 entrants for a gruelling trial of endurance, guts and skill. Check the local newspapers for details of the route.

Horse Racing. Race meetings take place once or twice a week from mid-September to the end of June (Saturdays or Sundays) at the Nicosia Racecourse in Ayios Dhometios.

Want a change from the beach? Why not try a scenic trek inland?

Shopping

From the sophisticated shops of Nicosia and Limassol to the kiosks set up along the roadside, you'll find plenty to tempt you in Cyprus. Most businesses open from 8 a.m. to 1 p.m. and 4 to 7 p.m. weekdays (mornings only on Wednesdays and Saturdays). Larger hotels usually have good boutiques stocked with limited selections of everything from clothing and souvenirs to jewellery.

Best Buys

Cypriots are wonderful artisans, renowned for their handicrafts—ceramics, wood-carving, weaving, basketry, silver and copper work. The Cyprus Handicraft Service (C.H.S.), a non-profit organization, runs shops with a good selection of items in Nicosia, Limassol, Larnaca and Paphos.

Basketry. The choice ranges from small portable baskets in decorative shapes and colours to large pieces in rush or cane.

Brass. Look for candlesticks, ashtrays, small boxes, religious souvenirs and trays.

Carpets and curtains. In Cypriot patterns, with a Near-Eastern and Turkish influence, these can be colourful and in good taste. The woollen rugs in all sizes are very tempting.

Ceramics. Many artisans look back to antiquity for inspiration, creating charming animal figurines, little vessels and terracotta statuettes, fashioned by hand and fired. The functional wares of Kornos and Phini include attractive hand-thrown wine and oil jars. Glazed ceramics may have very pretty geometric patterns in the Cypriot style.

Copperware. Dating from over 3,000 years ago, the copper industry remains a source of Cypriot pride. You'll see all manner of hand-crafted ware, including copper pots, saucepans and bowls.

Embroidery. Shops all over Cyprus sell the island's most important cottage industry item —fine linen tablecloths, doilies, runners and handkerchiefs stitched with the intricate geometric patterns of Lefkara (see p. 48).

Food and wine. Turkish Delight *(loukhoumi)* is a speciality of Yeroskipos and Lefkara—though shops all over sell it. You may want to carry home Cypriot olives or sealed packets of the local cheese, *halloumi.* Of the many wines and liqueurs produced on Cyprus, you might purchase some Commandaria, the sweet red dessert wine—it comes in decorative bottles of various sizes.

Jewellery. Silver, gold and filigreed pieces make interesting buys. Be sure to get a certificate of authenticity from the jeweller for important costly purchases.

Leather goods. Manufactured locally, shoes and sandals are reasonably priced and well-styled on Cyprus, especially models for women. Appealing presents for yourself and others include hand-tooled handbags, belts and wallets—as well as soft leather jackets, waistcoats (vests), skirts and trousers.

Souvenirs. Gifts with a local touch range from colourful Cypriot stamps and stamp gift booklets (at larger post offices), coins and maps, to records and cassettes of Cypriot music.

Wooden articles. Craftsmen produce everything from elaborate picture-frames to traditional Cypriot-style dowry chests. At the Nicosia outlet of the Cyprus Handicrafts Service you can order custom-made furniture, to be shipped home.

Woollen goods. Heavy patterned sweaters, tie belts and shawls have a rustic appeal. Woollen shoulder bags are another speciality.

Woven Goods. Colourful, hand-loomed fabrics made up into dresses, children's clothing and shirts for men and women **92** need not be expensive.

Nightlife

After dark, Aphrodite's island seems to wind down to an early bedtime, unless you know where to go.

For drinking and music, you can prowl around at portside in Larnaca, Limassol and Paphos, where cafés and bars, *souvlaki* and fish restaurants go full-swing late into the evening. Strolling musicians occasionally liven up the night scene at quaysides and in colourful tavernas.

Nicosia, Limassol, Paphos and Larnaca have discothèques, snack bars with music and *bouzouki* places, where spectators are invited to join in when there is Greek dancing. But Limassol's cabarets provide the liveliest night out, keeping the Arab and Lebanese colony there entertained until the wee hours.

Most hotels offer weekly folklore shows with Cypriot-costumed performers singing and dancing to charming village tunes. It's all in good fun, you're invariably encouraged to get up and dance along—and nobody objects to missteps. Hotels also organize special buffets and cocktail parties, gaming nights and fashion shows.

The Nicosia Municipal Theatre stages plays in Greek and sometimes English; concerts are held here, too. Films in English are shown in the larger cities. Ask at your hotel or consult local papers and *Cyprus Time Out* for information about special events.

A Cyprus-by-night tour might take you to a local restaurant to sample *mezedes* and on to a performance of traditional Cypriot dancing with *bouzouki* music. Some tours include an amusing pastiche of a Cypriot wedding in full swing.

Otherwise, should evening restlessness set in, follow the path of Aphrodite: if you're near the sea, walk down to the shore, watch the moon if there is one visible and listen to the waves. A moonlight walk in the mountains to breathe the tonic air and listen to the wind in the pines can be just as romantic—a welcome change from the frantic blast of a night club.

Festivals and Holy Days

Listed below are just a few of the principal events, as every town commemorates its patron saint, from Luke to Neophytos. Feast days and other holidays bring out the inevitable merchants and their stands *(paniyiri)* of market produce, sweets, drinks and trinkets.

January	*Ta Fota.* On Epiphany Day (January 6), bishops bless the waters in all the seaside towns, throwing their Holy Crosses in. Boys often dive for them, winning a small prize when they surface with one after an icy dive.
February/ March	*Clean Monday.* Large amounts of vegetables, olives and wine are consumed on this day of "fasting", the Monday before Lent.
	Carnival. Limassol's ten-day-long celebration features fancy-dress balls and a spate of parades. It's not Rio, but it's light-hearted.
March/April	*Good Friday.* Orthodox Solemn Masses take place all over Cyprus, with a procession of the Holy Sepulchre in main streets and squares.
	Easter. A midnight service takes place on the Saturday before Easter, when people light their candles from the priest's, moving around the church and chanting the litany in a kind of sound-and-light atmosphere that is nevertheless fervently religious. On Easter Sunday, High Masses celebrate the resurrection of Christ. The rest of the day is devoted to socializing, eating and games.
May/June	*Kataklismos.* Also known as Pentecost, this two-day holiday harks back to ancient times, when Cypriots convened at temples to worship and sacrifice to Adonis and Aphrodite, continuing their celebrations down at the seashore. Nowadays there are excursions to the beach, colourful parades, parties, games, competitions and "dousing"—especially at Paphos.
August	*Assumption of the Virgin.* On August 15, the faithful gather at the leading monasteries: Kykko, Chrysorroyiatissa, Troodhitissa, Macheras. (Beware of crowds: the small roads leading to the churches can be clogged with cars.)
	Lefkara Festival. In mid-August, Lefkara holds a village festival to display its famous embroidery and

other crafts. There's music, dancing and food stands galore.

September

The Virgin Nativity. On September 8, a crowd assembles at Kykko Monastery to observe all the attendant rites, from icon-kissing to lemonade-drinking.

Nicosia Arts Festival. This two-week-long event features everything from art exhibitions and folk dancing to avant-garde ballet and rock concerts. Most of the events take place in the historic Famagusta Gate Cultural Centre.

Limassol Wine Festival. A fortnight of wine-tastings, dancing, folklore shows and a bit of carefree drunkenness liven up the sedate public gardens.

Platres Festival. The Troodos village of Pano Platres mounts an annual exhibition of local crafts.

Eating Out

Take some exotic tastes from the Near East, mix with fresh produce and add big dashes of colour: that's what the best Cypriot cooking is all about—especially in the grand arrays of *mezedes* found in many hotels and restaurants. The food of Cyprus has much in common with that of Greece, but Turkish and other influences have made it more exciting.

A feast of food and wine at a hotel in Pano Platres.

With tourism on the rise, that hybrid called "international cuisine" has raised its boring head, with some bland pap occasionally replacing real, local food. And British-style fish-and-chips is being overtaken by the ubiquitous hamburger and pizza. But take heart: such local fast-food items as pitta bread with *sheftalia* (a kind of sausage) and *souvlaki* (skewered meat) are not yet mass-produced and the quality can be high.

As opposed to Greece, where you're encouraged to rush in to the kitchen to point out what you'd like to eat, Cyprus restaurants usually expect you to

order from the menu (almost invariably translated into English and perhaps other languages), with the waiter's help.

In Mediterranean fashion, local people tend to eat late (from 1.30 to 3.30 p.m. for lunch, 9 to 10.30 p.m. for dinner). But service begins an hour or even two hours before the times given above. Things are quieter, but you'll usually get good service if you come early—also a good idea if you're eating with young children.

As Cyprus produces excellent wine, beer and brandy, reasonably priced drinks before, during or after meals can contribute to the general euphoria.

Photo: Suzanne Patterson.

Breakfast

The usual hotel breakfast is Continental: rolls, toast or bread, biscuits and perhaps croissants with butter and jam, and coffee, tea or chocolate. The tea will probably be made from bags, and the coffee is all too often an envelope or two of instant powder with hot water, to be concocted to taste.

For big appetites, some hotels offer an English-style breakfast of ham and eggs, perhaps porridge or kippers. Some international hotel menus also list American-style breakfast cereals. Fresh fruits and fruit juices are almost always available and delicious.

Those who prefer real coffee should order the "Greek" or "Turkish" variety, readily available at any time of day in cafés or tavernas. Order it sweet *(gliko)*, medium sweet *(metrio)*, or without sugar *(sketo)*. Greek coffee is taken black, never with cream or sugar, and is usually accompanied by a glass of ice water.

Starters

Hot and cold appetizers *(mezedes)* can be so varied and interesting that you could make a whole meal of them. Some restaurants offer menus of over 20 items. Naturally, in this food cornucopia you'll find Greek- **97** style *taramosalata* (fish-roe paste with oil, mashed potato or softened bread and lemon juice). *Dzadziki* (yoghurt with cucumber, crushed garlic and seasonings) is well known as a Greek or Turkish dish, but probably originated in Lebanon. *Talattouri,* a Cypriot variant of this preparation, will invariably be seasoned with fresh mint. Other popular dips include *tachinosalata* (sesame seed paste with garlic) and *hoummmous,* a purée of chickpeas, olive oil and hot spices. To accompany these dips, you'll be served fresh Cypriot sesame-seed *(koulouri)* bread, which has a hearty homemade taste, and may be toasted.

The array of *mezedes* continues with *melidzanosalata* (aubergine—eggplant—puréed with oil, garlic, a little vinegar, lemon juice and seasonings) and a small plate of black olives. You may be served a tomato salad, pickled capers and cauliflower *(moungra)* or spicy squid or octopus *(ktapodhi ksidhato),* cut into small pieces.

Smoked sausages figure prominently among *mezedes* offerings, whether *sheftalia* (pork, veal or lamb) or the ever-popular pork and beef *loukanika.* There's succulent marinated ham, pressed *(chiromeri)* or smoked *(lounza),* and smoked fillet of pork, charcoal-grilled or cold and thin-sliced. Don't pass up *halloumi,* Cypriot ewe's milk cheese, which may be served hot (grilled or fried) or cold. *Dolmadakia* are the well-known vine leaves stuffed with rice, lamb and sometimes mint.

Souvlakia, skewered pieces of lamb (or chicken, beef or pork) grilled over charcoal, may be eaten as a starter or a main course—as may grilled lamb chops.

Soups and Pasta

Order hearty mixed vegetable, pea or lentil soup or the appealing *avgolemono,* a lemon-flavoured chicken broth thickened with egg and served with rice, of Greek origin. *Trachanas,* a healthy speciality, combines cracked wheat and yoghurt.

Fresh pasta—excellent and popular on Cyprus—may mean fettucini or tagliatelli with meat, cream or vegetable sauces. Be sure to try *kypriakes ravioles,* Cypriot ravioli stuffed with *halloumi* (ewe's milk cheese), eggs and mint.

Fish and Shellfish

Since offshore catches are relatively scanty, the choice of seafood may be limited. Shrimp, squid and spiny lobster appear on menus, but it's likely they will be frozen, rather than fresh. However, you may be offered fresh swordfish *(xifias),* red mullet *(barbounia),* red snapper *(sinagrida)* or a small Mediterranean fish called *psirika.* These varieties may be grilled, sautéed, stuffed and baked or, more rarely, cooked in a wine sauce. Some hotel chefs prepare mixed shellfish salads (mussels, shrimp, spiny lobster), and they can be excellent. In the Troodos mountains the farm-raised trout are very good whether smoked, sautéed, perhaps with slivered almonds, or *au bleu* (poached with drawn butter).

Meat and Vegetables

Cypriots love the ubiquitous *moussaka* as much as Greeks do; this layered dish of minced meat, aubergine (eggplant) and marrows (squash), potatoes, cream sauce and spices varies somewhat, according to the chef. A slightly different taste and texture characterize aubergine stuffed with minced meat and tomatoes and topped with beaten egg and breadcrumbs *(papoutsakia). Stifado,* beef or veal stew, usually contains wine, onions and herb seasoning. *Patcha* is sheep's head stewed with lemon and garlic. Chicken *(kotopoulo)* may be barbecued, roasted, or served in a casserole with sauce, and perhaps mushrooms and onions as well.

A variety of plain grilled steaks and chops feature on all menus. Lamb is cooked in a kind of clay pot with vegetables and spices *(tavas)* or cut into chops and kebabs and barbecued *(kleftiko).* Pork and suckling pig can be delicious grilled (perhaps over charcoal) or roasted. Look out for *aphelia,* a tender pork stew made with red wine and coriander seeds, which does not often appear on hotel or restaurant menus.

Vegetable dishes and accompaniments include black-eyed beans *(louvia),* potatoes, rice, green beans or peas, tomatoes, courgettes (zucchini) and aubergines. Fresh green salads are always available. "Greek" or "village-style" salads incorporate onions, olives, peppers, tomatoes and *feta* cheese. In hotels and at poolsides you'll see mixed chef's salad, potato, egg and *Niçoise* salads.

Desserts

Cheese offerings are limited to the local ewe's milk *halloumi* (salty and mild), Greek-style *feta* (a bit stronger) and some rather tired imports. Sometimes *graviera* is served—a local version of Swiss *gruyère*—as well as *kefalotyri* and *kaskavalli.*

Concentrate instead on the fruit of Cyprus. Depending on the season, you'll be able to try the outstanding honeydew or cantaloupe melon, watermelon, cherries, peaches, apricots, oranges, tangerines, plums, figs, grapes, pomegranates, and more... You may also find wonderful yoghurt and honey, though not so often as in Greece.

Cypriot sweets are very sweet indeed. A speciality of Yeroskipos and Lefkara, *loukhoumi* is the sugar-dusted, jellied Turkish Delight. Honey and nuts flavour *baklava,* a strudel-like pastry, and *kataifi,* a pastry which resembles shredded wheat. Another speciality of Cypriot pastry chefs, *loukoumades* are a kind of very sweet puffy doughnut dipped in syrup. The ice-cream, ices and sundaes can be excellent, and many hotels offer French-style pastries and tarts.

Drinks

In addition to a variety of soft drinks and mineral water, you'll find excellent beer, brewed in Cyprus. Like the Greeks, Cypriots favour *ouzo,* the refreshing anis-flavoured apéritif. Poolside drinks often include cooling Pimm's cup; and don't miss the heady, fruit brandy sours—which are to

Cyprus what *piña colada* is to the Caribbean. Otherwise all the usual cocktails and drinks are available, and on the expensive side when they include imported spirits.

Wines

Cyprus wines have been renowned since antiquity. Foremost among them is the sweet, red Commandaria, originally produced for the Knights of St. John at Kolossi. It's celebrated as an apéritif or dessert wine, and worth trying even if you usually eschew sweet wines. Sweet to dry wines of the sherry type are another Cypriot speciality.

Drinking in the glorious setting of Paphos Harbour.

Constantly improving, Cypriot table wines equal the best similar vintages of Italy and Spain, and even some of the lesser wines of France. White wines are usually quite light but not sweet; the outstanding names include Keo Hock, White Lady, Aphrodite and Arsinoë. Bella Pais, a rather bubbly white, makes a good apéritif or dessert wine. Duc de Nicosie is the "champagne" of Cyprus (made according to true Champagne methods).

Red wines are catching up to whites in quality and popularity—even in this warm climate. Keo Claret, Olympus Claret and Domaine d'Ahera in particular often have subtlety as well as body. Othello, a very well-known brand, can be outstanding (but not cheap) in vintage years—try the banner year of 1959. There are a few rosés; most people consider Cœur de Lion the best.

For an after-dinner drink, try some Cypriot brandy. In the more sophisticated category, Five Kings is one of the better-known brands. Filfar, a very strong liqueur, resembles Grand Marnier in taste.

How to Get There

From Great Britain

Direct daily flights link London to Larnaca, and there is service twice weekly from Manchester. The fares available include first, business and economy class, as well as two excursion fares, valid seven to 90 days. One allows for stopovers, while the other carries a reduction for night travel.

Charter flights and package tours: Tour operators offer a wide variety of packages originating in London. The price includes air travel (on a group fare basis), transfers and either hotel or apartment accommodation, the former with or without meals. Car hire at discounted rates is optional.

By boat: Car-ferries run at regular intervals between Venice and Limassol, a journey of four days. Meals are included in the price.

From North America

Connecting service operates to Larnaca from New York, Miami, Los Angeles and San Francisco. In addition to first, business and economy class, there is the more economical excursion fare, valid for 14 days to four months. The APEX (Advance Purchase Excursion) fare, good for six days to two months, must be booked 14 days in advance. A reduction is made for APEX travel during the winter months. Children up to age 12 can fly for a discount, and there is a special youth fare for young people 12 through 24. Youth fare tickets may be booked no sooner than five days before the outward and return flights.

From the Southern Hemisphere

Australia: Most travellers to Cyprus fly via Athens. An excursion fare (valid ten days to four months) is offered on this route. Passengers may make one stop in each direction.

New Zealand: The most direct route to Larnaca is via Sydney and Athens. (See under Australia for details of the excursion fare.)

South Africa: The usual routing to Larnaca involves changing planes in Lusaka or Athens. The excursion fare (good six days to three months) allows a total of three stops en route.

When to Go

Year-round Cyprus boasts sunny skies and low humidity. On the coast, sea breezes temper the heat of July and August, though the thermometer has been known to hit 38 °C (100 °F) in Nicosia, inland. Citizens of the capital beat a quick retreat to the coast or Troodos resorts during the dog days of summer.

January and February see snow falls in the Troodos range—enough most years to allow for some skiing. It rains occasionally between October and February, but there's plenty of sun, too, and the sea remains warm enough for some brisk bathing.

Days of sun (sea coast): 340

Average daytime temperature in Nicosia:

		J	F	M	A	M	J	J	A	S	O	N	D
Maximum	°C	15	16	19	24	29	34	37	37	33	28	22	17
	°F	59	61	66	75	85	92	98	98	92	83	72	63
Minimum	°C	5	5	7	10	14	18	21	21	18	14	10	7
	°F	42	42	44	50	58	65	70	69	65	58	51	45

Planning Your Budget

To give you an idea of what to expect, here are some average prices in Cypriot pounds (CY£). However, take into account that all prices must be regarded as approximate, due to the rise in inflation.

Airport transfer. Taxi to Larnaca town CY£1.25, to Nicosia CY£8–9; shared taxi to Nicosia CY£1, to Limassol CY£1.20.

Baby-sitters. About CY£1.25 per hour.

Bicycle and motorcycle hire. Bicycles CY£1–1.75 per day, motorcycles CY£2.50–10 per day.

Buses. Larnaca town–Nicosia CY£0.55, Larnaca town–Limassol CY£0.65, Limassol–Pano Platres CY£0.60.

Camping. From CY£1–1.25 per day for tent or caravan plus CY£0.25–0.28 per person per day for services and taxes. Caravans (trailers) can be rented from CY£7–8 per day, plus delivery charges.

Car hire. Rates per day for 1–6 days in summer season (unlimited mileage): *Austin Mini* CY£13, *Ford Escort* CY£13, *Opel Kadett* CY£14.50, *Subaru* CY£16.10, *Mini-bus* CY£20.60.

Cigarettes. Foreign brands manufactured under licence in Cyprus CY£0.40 per packet, imported CY£0.80 per packet.

Entertainment. Cinema CY£1; discotheque (admission and one drink) from CY£2; cabaret (admission, drink, show and dancing) from CY£2.

Hairdressers. *Man's* haircut (with wash) CY£2.50. *Woman's* shampoo and set or blow-dry CY£2.50–3, permanent wave CY£10–15.

Guides. CY£13.50 per half-day, CY£20.60 per day, 50% more on Sundays, 100% on public holidays.

Hotels. Double room with bath: 5-star CY£27–51, 4-star CY£18–30, 3-star CY£13–22, 2-star CY£10–16, one-star CY£8–11.

Meals and drinks. Continental breakfast CY£1.30–1.50, lunch or dinner in fairly good establishment CY£1.50–5, coffee CY£0.20–0.40, soft drinks CY£0.15–0.25, glass of wine or beer CY£0.30–0.50, brandy sour CY£0.75, gin and tonic CY£0.80.

Sports. Use of hotel beach facilities and/or tennis courts CY£1–3 per half hour; water-skiing CY£7.50 per half hour, windsurfing CY£3 per hour, sailing CY£4–5 per hour, motor boats CY£6 per hour or CY£25 per day.

Taxis. Initial charge CY£0.25, plus CY£0.23 per mile in towns (CY£0.17 for a return trip). Minimum charge CY£0.50.

BLUEPRINT for a Perfect Trip

An A-Z Summary of Practical Information and Facts

> Listed after some basic entries is the appropriate Greek expression, usually in the singular, plus a number of phrases that should help you when seeking assistance. Accent marks are given to indicate stress.
> For all prices, refer to list on p. 102.

Contents

A **AIRPORTS** (ΑΕΡΟΔΡΟΜΙΟ—*aerodrómio*). Larnaca International Airport, the principal air gateway to Cyprus, lies 3½ miles from Larnaca town and 30 miles from Nicosia. Taxis are available for the trip into both cities, while shared taxis and mini-buses, scheduled frequently during the day, provide inexpensive transport for three or more passengers. A few local buses operate daily to Larnaca and Limassol.

A replacement for Nicosia airport—since 1974 on United Nations territory and no longer used for commercial flights—the Larnaca facility has been modernized and expanded to cope with increased air traffic into the Republic of Cyprus. Larnaca has a duty-free shop, snack bar, restaurant, currency-exchange, car hire agencies, post office and tourist information office. Check-in counters may be crowded and service somewhat slow, so arrive with plenty of time to spare (at least 1½ hours) before flight departure.

Paphos International Airport, 7 miles north-east of Paphos town on the west coast, handles freight and certain scheduled and charter services, easing the congestion at Larnaca. Paphos has a duty-free shop, currency-exchange facilities and restaurants.

The airport at Ercan in north Cyprus, served by flights from the mainland of Turkey only, is not recognized by the Republic of Cyprus as a legal point of entry.

Porter! Take these bags to the bus/taxi, please.	**Parakaló! Pigénete aftés tis aposkevés sto leoforío/taxí.**

ALPHABET. See also LANGUAGE. Signs in Cypriot towns and cities usually appear in Greek and English. But in the villages, a familiarity with Greek can be useful.

The exotic letters of the Greek alphabet needn't be a mystery to you. The table below lists the Greek letters in their capital and small forms, followed by the letter they correspond to in English.

A	α	a	as in bar		H	η	i	like **ee** in meet
B	β	v			Θ	θ	th	as in **thin**
Γ	γ	g	as in go*		I	ι	i	like **ee** in meet
Δ	δ	d	like **th** in **this**		K	κ	k	
E	ε	e	as in get		Λ	λ	l	
Z	ζ	z			M	μ	m	

106 ———— *except before **i**- and **e**-sounds, when it's pronounced like **y** in yes

N	ν	n		Y	υ	i	like **ee** in meet
Ξ	ξ	x	like **ks** in thanks	Φ	φ	f	
O	o	o	as in b**o**ne	X	χ	ch	as in Scottish lo**ch**
Π	π	p		Ψ	ψ	ps	as in ti**ps**y
P	ρ	r		Ω	ω	o	as in b**o**ne
Σ	σ, ς	s	as in ki**ss**	OY	ου	ou	as in s**ou**p
T	τ	t					

A

ANTIQUITIES *(antíkes)*. The purchase and export of antiquities is strictly regulated, and export permission must be granted by the Director of the Department of Antiquities, c/o Ministry of Communications and Works, Nicosia. It is illegal to remove antiquities, stones and other remains from any archaeological site, including the seabed.

BABY-SITTERS. The personnel at your hotel reception desk will be glad to arrange for a sitter if you give one or two days' notice. Failing that, you may also find a sitter through advertisements in local English-language magazines and papers.

B

Can you get me a baby-sitter for tonight?
Boríte na mou vríte mía "baby-sitter" giapópse?

BICYCLE and MOTORCYCLE HIRE (ΕΝΟΙΚΙΑΣΕΙΣ ΠΟΔΗΛΑΤΩΝ—*enikiásis podiláton;* ΕΝΟΙΚΙΑΣΕΙΣ ΜΟΤΟΣΥΚΛΕΤΤΩΝ— *enikiásis motosiklettón*). You can hire bicycles and motorscooters or motorcycles from agencies in Nicosia, Limassol, Larnaca, Paphos, Ayia Napa and Polis. To operate a motorscooter or motorcycle, you must be at least 18 years of age and the holder of a driver's licence. The use of a crash helmet is obligatory.

CAMPING (ΚΑΜΠΙΝΓΚ—*"camping"*). Official campsites are licensed by the government. Most provide full comforts, including electricity, toilets and showers, washing facilities, café-restaurant and food shop. The main sites are at Troodos; Polis (30 miles north of Paphos); Forest Beach, east of Larnaca; Ayia Napa, near the village. The government permits a few other sites to operate on a provisional basis, especially those with basic facilities near restaurants.

C

Several firms in Nicosia and Limassol hire out caravans (trailers) for reasonable prices, with delivery to the various campsites.

C Inquire about all facilities and possibilities listed above at the nearest Cyprus Tourism Organization office (see p. 124). For local, unlisted campsites, ask at the police station in the nearest town.

Is there a campsite nearby?	**Ipárchi éna méros giá "camping" edó kondá?**
We have a caravan (trailer).	**Échoume trochóspito.**

CAR HIRE (ΕΝΟΙΚΙΑΣΕΙΣ ΑΥΤΟΚΙΝΗΤΩΝ—*enikiásis aftokiníton*). See also DRIVING. International and local car hire firms have offices in the major cities, as well as representatives at Larnaca and Paphos airports and at the main hotels. Rates are not cheap, but if you rent from a better-known local firm, you'll generally get good value. Some Cyprus firms charge slightly less than international agencies and provide equally good cars and service. Ask about reduced rates for weekly or monthly rentals. Note that the rate always includes unlimited mileage.

Reserve a car ahead of time—especially for the high (summer) season, when there often are not enough rental vehicles to go around. Air conditioning and automatic transmission are the exception rather than the rule; make any special requests in advance.

To hire a car, you must have a valid national licence (held at least one year) or an International Driving Permit. Depending on the company, the minimum age is 21 to 25. A deposit is usually required unless you pay by credit card, accepted by the larger firms.

I'd like to hire a car (tomorrow).	**Tha íthela na nikiáso éna aftokínito (ávrio).**
for one day/a week	**giá mía iméra/mía evdomáda**
Please include full insurance.	**Sas parakaló na simberilávete miktí asfália.**

CIGARETTES, CIGARS, TOBACCO *(tsigára; poúra; kapnós).* As there are no special tobacconist's shops, smokers usually step into general stores selling gifts, magazines and sundries to find what they're seeking. International brands produced under licence in Cyprus can be purchased at very low prices; imported tobacco products cost approximately twice as much.

A packet of .../A box of matches, please.	**Éna pakéto .../Éna koutí spírta, parakaló.**
filter-tipped	**me fíltro**
without filter	**chorís fíltro**

CLIMATE and CLOTHING. In summer, follow Mediterranean practice and wear comfortable loose cotton clothing (synthetics are unsuitable in this climate). Nights can be cool, even in summer, so be sure to pack a sweater or jacket. In winter months (late November to March), you'll need a raincoat or light winter coat, a warm sweater or jacket, and perhaps a woollen outfit or two.

On the beach toplessness is generally tolerated, although Cypriot women don't often go topless themselves; nudity in public is unacceptable. Take along a cover-up for the beach-bar—not just for modesty, but for the cool breezes that blow up.

Informality is the general rule, but in many hotels and restaurants people do dress up in the evening. So you may want to take something besides jeans and minimal sportswear: attractive dresses and skirts or trousers for women, jacket and tie for men. Women find knee-length skirts both cool and appropriate for visits to Orthodox churches and monasteries; men should wear long trousers and shirts.

COMMUNICATIONS. (See also Hours.)

Post offices (ΤΑΧΥΔΡΟΜΕΙΟ—*tachidromío*). All branches handle mail, but only the larger offices provide full telex and telegram services. In Nicosia, the central post office is situated in Eleftheria Square.

If you don't know ahead of time where you'll be staying, have your mail sent poste restante (general delivery).

Telephone and telegrams *(tiléfono; tilegráfima).* Telephone and telegram communications come under the auspices of the Cyprus Telecommunications Authority (CYTA). Automatic service operates for local, long-distance and international calls. The direct-dialling codes to main Cypriot cities are:

Nicosia	021	Larnaca	041
Limassol	051	Paphos	061

Telephone Spelling Code			
A Aléxandros	**H** Iraklís	**N** Nikólaos	**T** Timoléon
B Vasílios	**Θ** Theódoros	**Ξ** Xenofón	**Y** Ipsilántis
Γ Geórgios	**I** Ioánnis	**O** Odisséfs	**Φ** Fótios
Δ Dimítrios	**K** Konstantínos	**Π** Periklís	**X** Chrístos
E Eléni	**Λ** Leonídas	**P** Ródos	**Ψ** Psáltis
Z Zoí	**M** Menélaos	**Σ** Sotírios	**Ω** Oméga

C In better hotels you can dial long-distance from your room, but a surcharge may be added to the bill. Standard rates and other information are available from the long-distance operator (194).

For local calls, most cafés, newspaper kiosks and food shops will allow you to use their phones.

Where's the (nearest) post office/ telephone office?	**Pou íne to kodinótero tachidromío/CYTA?**
Have you received any mail for...?	**Échete grámmata giá...?**
A stamp for this letter/ postcard, please.	**Éna grammatósimo giaftó to grámma/graftí tin kárta, parakaló.**
express (special delivery)	**exprés**
airmail	**aeroporikós**
registered	**sistiméno**
I want to send a telegram to...	**Thélo na stílo éna tilegráfima sto...**
Can you get me this number in...?	**Boríte na mou párete aftó ton arithmó...?**
reverse-charge (collect) call	**plirotéo apó to paralípti**
person-to-person (personal) call	**prosopikí klísi**

COMPLAINTS. They don't often arise in this hospitable country, but should you have any problems, speak to the manager or proprietor of the establishment in question. Your complaints will usually receive prompt and efficient attention, since most Cypriots are anxious to please.

CONSULATES and EMBASSIES (ΠΡΟΞΕΝΕΙΟ—*proxenío;* ΠΡΕΣΒΕΙΑ—*presvía*).

Australia	Chancery, 4 Annis Comnenis Street, Nicosia; tel. (021) 73001.
United Kingdom	High Commission, Alexander Pallis Street, Nicosia; tel. (021) 73131.
U.S.A.	Embassy, Disotheon and Therissou Streets, Lycavitos, Nicosia; tel. (021) 65151.

COURTESIES. See also MEETING PEOPLE. Among the sunniest, most
friendly people in the world, Cypriots are also unfailingly polite—

except occasionally behind the wheel of a car. Grounded, they offer to help, give directions and call taxis for you. **C**

Etiquette is informal, but it's customary to shake hands when greeting somebody or saying goodbye. Many Cypriots are so enthusiastic about visitors that even complete strangers unfailingly offer something to drink or eat, and you should try to accept. They love protracted conversations about anything from food to the state of the world, and they'll try to induce you to chat for a while, even if you're in a hurry. But time spent with Cypriots is rarely lost, since they're a great source of information about their country.

A few words of Greek from the visitor are appreciated but not really necessary; the polite phrases in English are just as welcome. Most people happily pose for photographs, and a copy sent to them makes a welcome thank you for a good holiday in their country.

CRIME and THEFT. There is still so little crime here that the few robberies per week or even month make headlines. Cypriots are generally honest, and the jail languishes for inmates. Unfortunately, this idyllic state of things may change fast, with the mass arrival of tourists and workers from nearby Mediterranean countries. Hoodlums from elsewhere simply don't observe the Cypriots' rules of honesty and fair play. So take the usual precautions of locking a car and stowing valuables in the boot (trunk), and of depositing money and jewellery in the hotel safe.

DRIVING **D**

Entering Cyprus. To bring your car into Cyprus you'll need:
- a valid driving licence or an International Driving Permit
- car registration papers
- a nationality plate or sticker

The green card is not valid in Cyprus, but it is compulsory to take out full third-party insurance coverage. Details are available at the port of entry or from the Registrar of Motor Vehicles:

24 Byron Avenue, Nicosia.

Cars may enter the country duty-free for up to six months.

For further information, you can also contact your local automobile association or the Cyprus Automobile Association:

30 Homer Avenue, Nicosia (tel. [021] 52521).

Speed limits are 30 miles per hour in towns, 50 mph on highways and 60 mph on motorways (expressways).

D **Driving conditions.** British motorists will feel at home in Cyprus, where traffic keeps to the left. Everyone else should go slow at first, until the habit of driving on the left, overtaking (passing) on the right becomes second nature. Use your horn if you need to, although it's officially prohibited in city centres after 9 p.m.

There are a few motorways (expressways)—notably the Nicosia-to-Limassol road, opened in 1984. Conditions on this superhighway are excellent, but beware of speeders. Otherwise, the larger roads are good to indifferent and the two-way thoroughfares often quite busy. Country roads may be mere cow paths, so you have to concentrate in case an animal or another car is coming from the opposite direction.

Although usually paved, "main" mountain roads can be treacherous: one and a half lanes for two-way traffic is the rule; they are often pockmarked with potholes and generally have steep, hairpin turns. Only the fittest, most alert drivers should attempt these roads.

Extreme caution is the best advice for drivers new to Cyprus, even on the motorways, since Cypriot drivers can be aggressive, know the roads and brook no interference—even though they, too, can have accidents. One hazard is narrow lanes and raised paved surfaces beside soft shoulders, making it very hard to keep on course if a large vehicle coming the other way should force you to the edge on a two-lane route. City traffic is fairly orderly (there are traffic lights in the larger cities), and you'll encounter only minor traffic jams in Nicosia.

Parking. It's no problem except in central Nicosia or perhaps a few crowded back streets in the old part of Larnaca. Fines may be handed out if you're in the way. Try to find a free or metered spot; there are car parks as well.

Fuel and oil. Prices are among the highest in Europe; diesel fuel proves somewhat less expensive, and you can rent diesel cars. Petrol stations are plentiful around Nicosia, Limassol and the coast, rather scarcer in the mountains. If you're setting out on an excursion, be sure the tank is full or nearly so, especially on Sundays or holidays, when many stations close. Petrol is sold by the gallon in Cyprus.

Road distances. Following are distances in miles between some major tourist centres in the Republic of Cyprus.

Nicosia–Limassol	54
Nicosia–Larnaca	32
Limassol-Paphos	48
Limassol-Troodos	36
Paphos–Ayia Napa (coast road)	114
Larnaca–Limassol	43

Breakdowns. Call your car hire agency, the Cyprus Automobile Association (tel. [021] 52521) or the police (tel. 199). **D**

Road signs. Most road signs are the standard pictographs used throughout Europe. However, you may encounter some written signs in English or Greek:

ΑΔΙΕΞΟΔΟΣ	No through road
ΑΛΤ	Stop
ΑΝΩΜΑΛΙΑ ΟΔΟΣΤΡΩΜΑΤΟΣ	Bad road surface
ΑΠΑΓΟΡΕΥΕΤΑΙ Η ΑΝΑΜΟΝΗ	No waiting
ΑΠΑΓΟΡΕΥΕΤΑΙ Η ΕΙΣΟΔΟΣ	No entry
ΑΠΑΓΟΡΕΥΕΤΑΙ Η ΣΤΑΘΜΕΥΣΙΣ	No parking
ΔΙΑΒΑΣΙΣ ΠΕΖΩΝ	Pedestrian crossing
ΕΛΑΤΤΩΣΑΤΕ ΤΑΧΥΤΗΤΑΝ	Reduce speed
ΕΠΙΚΙΝΔΥΝΟΣ ΚΑΤΩΦΕΡΕΙΑ	Dangerous incline
ΟΔΙΚΑ ΕΡΓΑ	Roadworks in progress (Men working)
ΚΙΝΔΥΝΟΣ	Caution
ΜΟΝΟΔΡΟΜΟΣ	One-way traffic
ΠΑΡΑΚΑΜΠΤΗΡΙΟΣ	Diversion (Detour)
ΠΟΔΗΛΑΤΑΙ	Cyclists
ΠΟΡΕΙΑ ΥΠΟΧΡΕΦΤΙΚΗ ΔΕΞΙΑ	Keep right
ΣΤΑΣΙΣ ΛΕΩΦΟΡΕΙΟΥ	Bus stop

(International) Driving Permit	**(diethnís) ádia odigíseos**
car registration papers	**ádia kikloforías**
collision insurance	**asfália enandíon trítou**
Can I park here?	**Boró na stathméfso edó?**
Are we on the right road for ...?	**Ímaste sto sostó drómo giá ...?**
Full tank, please— normal/super.	**Na to gemísete me venzíni aplí/soúper, parakaló.**
Check the oil/tires/battery.	**Na exetásete ta ládia/ta lásticha/ ti bataría.**
I've had a breakdown.	**Épatha mía vlávi.**
There's been an accident.	**Égine éna distíchima.**

ELECTRIC CURRENT. The standard current is 220/240 volts, 50 **E** cycles A.C.; sockets are usually three-prong, as in England. Adaptors are available in hotels and shops. Most hotels and blocks of flats have 110-volt outlets for razors.

I need an adaptor/a battery, please.	**Chriázome éna metaschimatistí/ mía bataría, parakaló.**

113

E **EMERGENCIES.** The following numbers are the ones to call in case of emergency.

Police, Fire Brigade, Ambulance (island-wide)		199
Hospital	Nicosia	51111
	Paphos	32364
	Larnaca	28120

These words are handy to know in difficult situations:

Careful	**Prosochí**	Police	**Astinomía**
Help	**Voíthia**	Stop	**Stamatíste**

ENTRY FORMALITIES and CUSTOMS CONTROLS. See also DRIVING. Most visitors, including British and American, need only a valid passport to enter Cyprus. European and North American visitors are not subject to any health requirements.

Legal points of entry are the ports of Larnaca, Limassol and Paphos and the international airports of Larnaca and Paphos. Visitors travelling via the airport of Ercan or the ports of Famagusta, Kyrenia or Karavostasi in the Turkish-controlled zone may not cross the border into the Republic of Cyprus.

The following chart shows what main duty-free items you may take into Cyprus and, upon your return home, into your own country:

Into:	Cigarettes	Cigars		Tobacco		Spirits		Wine
Cyprus	200	or	50	or	250 g.	¾ l.	or	2 l.
Australia	200	or	250 g. or		250 g.	1 l.	or	1 l.
Canada	200	and	50	and	900 g.	1.1 l.	or	1.1 l.
Eire	200	or	50	or	250 g.	1 l.	and	2 l.
N. Zealand	200	or	50	or	½ lb.	1 qt.	and	1 qt.
S. Africa	400	and	50	and	250 g.	1 l.	and	1 l.
U.K.	200	or	50	or	250 g.	1 l.	and	2 l.
U.S.A.	200	and	100	and	*	1 l.	or	1 l.
*A reasonable quantity								

Customs formalities are usually minimal, although there are sometimes long waits for passport control. Your luggage may be opened for inspection.

Currency restrictions. Travellers may import local currency up to CY£10. There is no limit on the amount of foreign currency you may bring into Cyprus, provided you declare it on arrival. You may export foreign currency up to the amount imported and declared. No more than CY£10 may be taken out of the country. **E**

I've nothing to declare.	**Den écho típota na dilóso.**
It's for my personal use.	**Íne giá prosopikí chrísi.**

GUIDES and INTERPRETERS *(xenagós; diermínéas)*. Professional, authorized guide-interpreters speaking English and other languages can be engaged through hotels and specialized agencies. **G**

We'd like an English-speaking guide.	**Tha thélame éna xenagó pou na milá angliká.**
I need an English interpreter.	**Chriázome éna ánglo diermínéa.**

HAIRDRESSERS (ΚΟΜΜΩΤΗΡΙΟ —*kommotírio*) **and BARBERS** (ΚΟΥΡΕΙΟ—*kourío*) It's easy to find hairdressing facilities of all categories—some salons are unisex. Naturally, prices are higher in the luxury hotel salons than in smaller, village shops, but everyone will try to please. Explain exactly what you want done. Somebody will invariably speak English, but in case you need to communicate in Greek, the following vocabulary will help: **H**

I'd like a shampoo and set.	**Tha íthela loúsimo ke miz-an-plí.**
I want a ...	**Thélo ...**
haircut	**koúrema**
blow-dry (brushing)	**chténisma me to pistoláki**
permanent wave	**mía permanád**
colour chart	**éna digmatológio**
colour rinse	**éna "shampoo" me chróma**
manicure	**mía manikioúr**
Don't cut it too short.	**Mi ta kópsete polí kondá.**
A little more off (here).	**Lígo pió kondá (edó).**

HEALTH and MEDICAL CARE. To be completely at ease, take out health insurance to cover any risk of illness and accident while on holiday. Your travel agent or insurance company at home will be able to advise you. (The Cyprus social services offer no free treatment to foreign visitors.) There are capable doctors and dentists in cities and larger towns, as well as adequate hospital facilities (see also **115**

H EMERGENCIES). All doctors are educated abroad and, in consequence, speak a second language, usually English.

Stomach upsets should not be a problem, as hotels and restaurants usually observe high standards of cleanliness. Tap water is safe to drink.

The wonderful sun rays can bronze you, but also burn you to a crisp. Take it in very easy doses at first (that means not more than 15 minutes a day towards spring and summer), and use a sun-screen cream, particularly if you have delicate skin.

Pharmacies (ΦΑΡΜΑΚΕΙΟ—*farmakío*) are recognized by the sign outside—a red cross on a white background (for hours, see p. 118). Certain chemists offer 24-hour service—check lists in local newspapers or ring a special information number (192). Most medicines sold in England, the United States and Canada or on the Continent are available, but often require a prescription. Pharmacists can generally advise on minor problems such as cuts, sunburn, blisters, throat infections and gastric disorders.

Where's the nearest (all-night) pharmacy?	**Pou íne to kondinótero (dianikterévon) farmakío?**
I need a doctor/dentist.	**Chriázome éna giatró/ odontogiatró.**
an ambulance	**éna asthenofóro**
hospital	**nosokomío**
I have	**Écho**
sunburn	**éngavma apó ton ílio**
sunstroke	**ilíasi**
a fever	**piretós**
an upset stomach	**varistomachiá**

HITCH-HIKING *(oto-stóp)*. Thumbing a ride is both legal and common on Cyprus, and people of all ages do it. However, whether you're a driver or hitch-hiker, use discretion.

Can you give me/us a lift to ...?	**Boríte na me/mas páte méchri to ...?**

HOTELS and ACCOMMODATION (ΞΕΝΟΔΟΧΕΙΟ; ΔΩΜΑΤΙΑ — *xenodochío; domátia*). See also CAMPING. In the high season (mid-June to October), try to book well in advance. The Cyprus Tourism **116** Organization (see p. 124) can furnish you with a brochure listing various possibilities in each town. If you arrive without a booking, contact the C.T.O. at the airport or in Nicosia, Larnaca, Limassol or Paphos for advice.

Cyprus has hotels of all categories, from five-star luxury havens to one-star bed-and-breakfast pensions, as well as very pleasant apartment-hotels (classified A and B) and clean, simple guest houses. In general, standards are high and prices are reasonable compared with other resorts and islands. Most hotels offer discounts during the low season, which for seaside resorts is from November 1 to March 31 (excluding the holiday period of December 20 to January 6) and for hill resorts from October 1 to June 30.

Youth hostels (ΞΕΝΩΝΑΣ ΝΕΩΝ—*xenónas néon*). Only members of the International Youth Hostels Association may stay at Cyprus's youth hostels:

Nicosia   13 Prince Charles Street (opposite Asty Hotel); tel. (021) 44808.

Paphos   E. Venizelos Avenue; tel. (061) 32588.

Troodos   Former Olympos Hotel (summer only); tel. (054) 15429.

Limassol   120 Ankara Street (behind Limassol Castle); tel. (051) 63749.

For further information contact the Cyprus Youth Hostels Association,

P.O. Box 1328, Nicosia, Cyprus.

Convents and **monasteries** frequently accept visitors for one or more nights, offering simple and clean accommodation with meals. For further information, contact the Cyprus Tourism Organization.

Villas may be rented through local agencies, or inquire at the C.T.O.

I'd like a single/double room.	**Tha íthela éna monó/dipló domátio.**
with bath/shower	**me bánio/dous**
What's the rate per night?	**Piá íne i timí giá mía níkta?**

HOURS

Archaeological sites. The major sites (Kolossi Castle, Curium, the Temple of Apollo, House of Dionysos mosaics, Tombs of the Kings at Paphos) remain open year-round from 7.30 a.m. until dusk, including Sundays and holidays, except Orthodox Easter Sunday.

H **Banks.** In general, hours are 8.30 a.m. to noon Monday to Saturday. Some banks in tourist centres open for currency exchange only from 3 to 5 p.m.

Museums. Opening hours vary according to city, season and type of museum. As a loose general rule, museums open weekdays and possibly on Saturdays from 7.30 or 8 a.m. to 1.30 or 2 p.m.; they close for a long lunch hour and open again from 3 to 5 or 4 to 6 p.m. Some institutions close on Sundays; others open from 10 a.m. to 1 p.m. The Cyprus Tourism Organization can furnish up-to-the-minute particulars.

Pharmacies. Except for the chemists on 24-hour duty, shops open from 7.30 or 8 a.m. to 1 p.m. and 3 or 4 to 7 p.m., Monday to Friday (morning only, Wednesday and Saturday).

Post offices. Most branches operate from 8 a.m. to 1.30 p.m. and 3 to 5 p.m. weekdays (mornings only, Saturday).

Restaurants. Lunch is normally served from 1.30 to 3.30 p.m. and dinner from 9 to 10.30 p.m.

Shops. Nearly all establishments do business from 8 a.m. to 1 p.m. and 4 to 7 p.m. weekdays (mornings only, Wednesday and Saturday).

L **LANGUAGE.** Greek Cypriots converse in a dialect that dates back to the time of Homer. With a distinctive vocabulary and pronunciation (the "ch" sound is strong), it is all but unintelligible to a Greek from the mainland. The written language, however, conforms to that of Greece.

In the country or the mountains, communication may be a problem, but invariably sign language saves the day. And everybody seems to know someone (a young student, perhaps) within shouting distance who can translate.

If you want to try Greek, consult the Berlitz phrase book GREEK FOR TRAVELLERS. It covers practically all the situations you're likely to encounter during your Cyprus travels.

Following are a few phrases you'll want to use often:

Good morning	**Kaliméra**	Please	**Parakaló**
Good afternoon	**Kalispéra**	Thank you	**Efcharistó**
Good night	**Kaliníkta**	Goodbye	**Chérete**

Do you speak English? **Miláte angliká?**
I don't speak Greek. **Den miló elliniká.**

LAUNDRY and DRY-CLEANING (ΠΛΥΝΤΗΡΙΟ—*plintírio;* ΣΤΕΓ-ΝΟΚΑΘΑΡΙΣΤΗΡΙΟ —*stegnokatharistírio*). Much of the year you can easily do your own small-article laundering; in the warm climate, clothes dry quickly. Otherwise, hotels and their maids are most efficient; some hotels offer one-day express service for an extra charge. Pressing can usually be done by afternoon if you give it in before 9 a.m. Otherwise, count two to three days for laundry and dry-cleaning. Some towns have launderette facilities and quick dry-cleaning services.

Where's the nearest laundry/dry-cleaners?	**Pou íne to kondinótero plintírio/stegnokatharistírio?**
When will it be ready?	**Póte tha íne étimo?**
I must have this for tomorrow morning.	**Prépi na íne étimo ávrio to proí.**

LOST PROPERTY. Cypriots are known for their honesty, and lost money or jewellery are often recovered by the owners. If you lose something, it will probably be kept for you at the place where you left it. Otherwise, inquire at the nearest police station.

Lost children will inevitably be taken care of. If you lose your child, tell people around you, then the police.

I've lost my wallet/handbag/passport.	**Échasa to portofóli mou/ti tsánda mou/to diavatirió mou.**

MAPS. The Cyprus Tourism Organization gives out comprehensive island maps and town plans of Nicosia, Limassol, Larnaca, Paphos and the Troodos region. Excellent for tourists, Clyde Surveys *A Leisure Map of Cyprus* indicates sights and sites, even hotel facilities available.

The maps in this book were prepared by Falk-Verlag, Hamburg.

I'd like a street plan of ...	**Tha íthela éna odikó chárti tis ...**
a road map of this region	**éna chárti aftís tis periochís**

MEETING PEOPLE. It's impossible *not* to meet people—what with all the smiling greetings, chit-chat, questions and interest about where you're from. Conversations with Cypriots or other tourists start casually anywhere—in shops, banks, tourist offices, hotels, museums, cafés—even simply asking directions. Cypriots are fascinated by **119**

M people from elsewhere. They also love to offer small presents—coffee, a drink, fruit, postcards. You should accept graciously.

As Cyprus is a Greek Orthodox country, manners and mores among the young are fairly regulated. But in cities, the older generation has given in to disco dancing and the cinema as a way of life. Young people can meet up in discos or at the beach, and young Cypriots are friendly. Young Cypriot men do not "pester" foreign girls, and foreign men should be equally discreet with Cypriot girls.

At any age, Cypriots show amazing warmth and friendliness, plus innate good manners. Smiles, thanks and goodbyes they give out in profusion. Visitors should really do the same.

How do you do?	**Ti kánete?**
How are you?	**Pos íste?**
Very well, thank you.	**Polí kalá, efcharistó.**

MONEY MATTERS (see also HOURS)

Currency. The Cyprus pound (CY£) is divided into 100 cents.
Coins: ½, 1, 2, 5, 10 and 20 cents.
Banknotes: 50 cents and CY£1, 5 and 10.
For currency restrictions, see ENTRY FORMALITIES AND CUSTOMS CONTROLS.

Currency exchange. Hotels change money and traveller's cheques, but banks (ΤΡΑΠΕΖΑ—*trápeza*) give much better rates—although the formalities can take a few minutes to half an hour.

Eurocheques, traveller's cheques, credit cards *("eurocheque", "traveller's cheque", pistotikí kárta).* Eurocheques are in widespread use in Cyprus. Traveller's cheques, widely accepted, are best cashed at a bank. Major credit cards are welcome as payment in most city shops, hotels, and restaurants, as well as by all the international and better local car hire firms. Don't forget to bring your passport along.

Cash. Dollars and other strong currencies may be accepted by shops or restaurants—but you'll probably get a poor exchange rate.

I want to change some pounds/ dollars.	**Thélo na alláxo merikés líres/ meriká dollária.**
Do you accept traveller's cheques?	**Pérnete "traveller's cheques"?**
Can I pay with this credit card?	**Boró na pliróso me aftí ti pistotikí kárta?**

NEWSPAPERS and MAGAZINES *(efimerída; periodikó).* There is a good selection of European periodicals and the major American weekly news magazines in larger towns. Foreign newspapers arrive one or two days after publication, depending on where you are. The *Cyprus Mail,* an English-language daily, has limited news reporting. The *Cyprus Weekly* (in English) carries lively features and helpful information. *Cyprus Time Out* is the publication to consult for listings of leisure events.

Have you any English-language newspapers?	**Échete anglikés efimerídes?**

PHOTOGRAPHY. Leading brands of film are usually available in Cyprus.

For security reasons, it is not allowed to photograph military installations—especially along the border of the Turkish-controlled zone. Although prohibitory signs are rarely posted, refrain from taking pictures in restricted areas.

Be sure to ask permission before using your camera in a museum.

I'd like some film for this camera.	**Tha íthela éna film giaftí ti michaní.**
black-and-white film	**asprómavro film**
colour prints	**énchromo film**
colour slides	**énchromo film giá thiafánies**
35-mm film	**éna film triánda pénde milimétr**
super-8	**soúper-októ**
How long will it take?	**Póte tha íne étimo?**
May I take a picture?	**Boró na páro mía fotografía?**

POLICE (ΑΣΤΥΝΟΜΙΑ—*astinomía*). You probably won't see many policemen, but they are around and they inevitably prove friendly and helpful. You'll recognize the traffic police by their spick-and-span white gloves and sleeves. The Port Police sport blue uniforms. Regular police wear blue in winter, khaki in summer and cruise around in dark blue and white police cars. Like most islanders, they usually speak some English.

Island-wide, the police emergency number is 199.

Where's the nearest police station?	**Pou íne to kondinótero astinomikó tmíma?**

P **PUBLIC HOLIDAYS** *(argíes).* In addition to their own national holidays, Cypriots also celebrate certain Greek holidays. Offices all over the country close on the following days. Shops remain open on certain holidays: inquire locally as to which ones.

Jan. 1	*Protochroniá*	New Year's Day
Jan. 6	*ton Theofaníon*	Epiphany
Jan. 19	*onomastikí eortí tou aimnístou proédrou, Archiepiskópou Makaríou tou trítou*	Name day of the late President, Archbishop Makarios III
March 25	*Ikostí Pémti Martíou (tou Evangelismoú)*	Greek Independence Day
Apr. 1	*Iméra enárxeos kipriakoú agónos giá tin anexartisía*	Cyprus Struggle Day*
May 1	*Protomagiá*	Labour Day
Aug. 3	*epétios tou thanátou tou Archiepiskópou Makaríou tou trítou*	Anniversary of the death of Archbishop Makarios III
Aug. 15	*Dekapendávgoustos (tis Panagías)*	Assumption Day
Oct. 1	*Iméra tis anexartisías tis Kíprou*	Cyprus Independence Day
Oct. 28	*Ikostí Ogdói Oktovríou*	*Óchi* ("No") Day, commemorating Greek defiance of Italian ultimatum and invasion of 1940.
Dec. 24	*paramoní Christougénnon*	Christmas Eve
Dec. 25	*Christoúgenna*	Christmas Day
Dec. 26	*epávrios ton Christougénnon*	Boxing Day
Movable dates:	*Katharí Deftéra*	1st Day of Lent: Ash Monday
	Megáli Paraskeví	Good Friday
	Deftéra tou Páscha	Easter Monday

Note: The dates on which the movable holidays are celebrated often differ from those in the West.

Are you open tomorrow?	**Íste aniktí ávrio?**

─────────

*Granted from year to year by decision of the Council of Ministers.

RADIO and TELEVISION *(rádio; tileórasi)*. CBC (Cyprus Broadcasting Corporation) airs programmes and news in English, plus a good selection of music, throughout the day. The BBC World Service transmits news, features and music daily from 6 a.m. to 2.15 a.m. The BFBS (British Forces Broadcasting Service) offers daily local and U.K. news bulletins and commentary, as well as music.

The Republic of Cyprus has only one television network. Foreign films and serials (usually in English, sometimes in other languages) are shown nightly beginning around 9 or 10 p.m. Short newscasts in Greek, Turkish and English are given from 6 to 6.30 p.m.

SIESTA. In summer, the siesta is sacred: everything grinds to a halt from about 2 p.m. for at least two hours. You'd be wise, too, to simply relax at the beach, at poolside or in your hotel room. In the exhausting heat, there's not much else to do. Many businesses keep summer hours from 7.30 a.m. until 2.30 or 3 p.m., when they close for the rest of the day.

TIME DIFFERENCES. The chart below shows the time difference between Cyprus and various cities in winter (GMT + 2). In summer Cypriot clocks are put forward one hour.

New York	London	**Cyprus**	Johannesburg	Sydney	Auckland
5 a.m.	10 a.m.	**noon**	noon	9 p.m.	11 p.m.

What time is it?   **Ti óra íne?**

TIPPING. Service charges are included in hotel, restaurant and taverna bills. But "a little extra" is always appreciated, especially for good service. Average tips:

Hotel porter, per bag	20–30 cents
Maid, per day	30–50 cents
Waiter/barman	5–10% (optional)
Taxi driver	10% (optional)
Tour guide (private)	around 10%
Tour guide (group tour)	from 50 cents per day
Hairdresser	10–15%

T **TOILETS** (ΑΠΟΧΩΡΗΤΗΡΙΑ—*apohoritíria*). Public conveniences exist in larger towns, but not in any great numbers. Museums often have clean facilities, and the ones on the government-run "tourist beaches" are excellent. Toilets are generally signalled in English and Greek, with graphic silhouettes designating men and women. If you use the facilities in cafés, restaurants and hotels, it is customary to buy at least a coffee in exchange.

Where are the toilets? **Pou íne ta apohoritíria?**

TOURIST INFORMATION OFFICES (*grafío plirophorión tourismoú*). The Cyprus Tourism Organization, or C.T.O. (*Kypriakós Organismós Tourismoú—K.O.T.*) is a gold-mine of information, and its offices are staffed with friendly people who readily field all your questions, and have brochures and maps to help you plan your trip.

United Kingdom 213 Regent Street, London, W1R 8DA; tel. (01) 734 9822.

U.S.A. 13 E. 40th Street, New York, NY 10016; tel. (212) 686-6016.

In Cyprus the C.T.O. maintains offices at Larnaca airport, open day and night (tel. [041] 54389) and in the major tourist centres:

Nicosia 35 Aristokyprou Street, Laiki Yitonia; tel. 44264.
Limassol 15 Spyrou Araouzou Street; tel. 62756.
Larnaca Democratias Square at Zenon Street; tel. 54322.
Paphos 3 Gladstone Street; tel. 32841.
  Airport; tel. (061) 368 33.

Where's the tourist office? **Pou íne to grafío tourismoú?**

TRANSPORT. Cyprus has no railway system and bus service is not always frequent or reliable. Private and shared taxis fill the transport gap.

Taxis (ΤΑΞΙ—*taxí*). Vehicles are metered and rates are low, making private taxis a favourite form of island transport. Many visitors, daunted by the difficult road conditions, travel around the island exclusively by taxi.

Shared taxis and mini-buses (ΕΠΙΒΑΤΙΚΑ ΤΑΞΙ—*epivatikó taxí*; ΜΙΚΡΑ ΠΟΥΛΜΑΝ —*mikrá poúlman*). Shared services run according to a schedule, carrying several passengers for a very reasonable fixed price. This is a great way to get around the island. Shared services operate frequently within towns as well as between them. You

can board a shared vehicle at a rank on the street or call for one by **T**
telephone (book in advance for a long trip). The numbers of the various
private companies are listed in the telephone directory. See under
"Taxi".

Boat services. Ask at the tourist office about boat excursions and
short cruises in Cypriot waters. The only legal seaports of entry at
present are Limassol, Larnaca and Paphos. The main port of entry is
Limassol, served by several ferry lines and cruise companies.

Where's the nearest bus stop?	**Pou íne o kondinóteros stathmós ton leoforíon?**
When's the next boat/bus to ...	**Póte févgi to epómeno plío/leoforío giá ...?**
I want a ticket to ...	**Thélo éna isitírio giá ...**
single (one-way)	**apló**
return (round-trip)	**me epistrofí**
first/second class	**próti/deftéra thési**
Will you tell me when to get off?	**Tha mou píte pou na katevó?**
Where can I get a taxi/ shared taxi/mini-bus?	**Pou boró na vro éna taxí/ epivatikó taxí/mikrá poúlman?**
May I have a place in this taxi for ...?	**Thélo mía thési se taxí giá ...?**
What's the fare to ...?	**Piá íne i timí giá ...?**

WATER *(neró).* Tap water is safe to drink and can be positively **W**
delicious in the Troodos mountains, where it comes fresh from the
springs. Still and fizzy mineral waters are bottled on Cyprus; imported
waters are often available as well.

a bottle of mineral water	**éna boukáli metallikó neró**
fizzy (carbonated)/still	**me/chorís anthrakikó**

WEIGHTS and MEASURES. Now as in the days of empire, Cypriots
calculate in miles and gallons. However, the basic units of weight are
the dram and oke standard in Turkey and Egypt. Neighbourhood
grocers and supermarket outlets alike weigh produce accordingly. To
confuse the issue, milk is sold by the litre and beer by the pint, while
petrol is pumped by the gallon.

100 drams = 11.2 ounces
1 oke = 2.8 pounds
400 drams = 1 oke

125

SOME USEFUL EXPRESSIONS

yes/no	ne/óchi
please/thank you	parakaló/efcharistó
excuse me/you're welcome	me sinchoríte/típota
where/when/how	pou/póte/pos
how long/how far	póso keró/póso makriá
yesterday/today/tomorrow	chthes/símera/ávrio
day/week/month/year	iméra/evdomáda/mínas/chrónos
left/right	aristerá/dexiá
up/down	epáno/káto
good/bad	kalós/kakós
big/small	megálos/mikrós
cheap/expensive	ftinós/akrivós
hot/cold	zestós/kríos
old/new	paliós/néos
open/closed	aniktós/klistós
here/there	edó/ekí
free (vacant)/occupied	eléftheri/krateméni
early/late	norís/argá
easy/difficult	éfkolos/dískolos
Does anybody here speak English?	Milá kanís angliká?
What does this mean?	Ti siméni aftó?
I don't understand.	Den katalavéno.
Please write it down.	Parakaló grápste to.
Is there an admission charge?	Prépi na plclróso ísodo?
Waiter, please!	Garsóni (garçon), parakaló!
I'd like ...	Tha íthela ...
How much is that?	Póso káni aftó?
Have you something less expensive?	Échete káti ftinótero?
What time is it?	Ti óra íne?
Just a minute.	Éna leptó.
Help me, please.	Voithíste me, parakaló.

126

Index

An asterisk (*) next to a page number indicates a map reference. Where there is more than one set of page references, the one in bold type refers to the main entry. For index to Practical Information, see p.105.